Your
Business School

Getting In
and Staying In

Books by Lawrence Graham

Your Ticket to Law School
Your Ticket to Medical or Dental School
Your Ticket to Business School
Conquering College Life
Ten Point Plan for College Acceptance
Jobs in the Real World

Your Ticket to Business School

Getting In and Staying In

by Lawrence Graham

Bantam Books
Toronto • New York • London • Sydney • Auckland

YOUR TICKET TO BUSINESS SCHOOL:
GETTING IN AND STAYING IN
A Bantam Book / March 1985

Library of Congress Cataloging in Publication Data

Graham, Lawrence,
    Your ticket to business school.

    Bibliography: p. 130
    1. Business education—United States—Handbooks,
manuals, etc. I. Title.
HF1131.G714   1985   650'.07'1173   84-91007
ISBN 0-553-34146-4 (pbk.)

Published simultaneously in the United States and Canada

PRINTED IN THE UNITED STATES OF AMERICA

O   0 9 8 7 6 5 4 3 2 1

To Uncle Searcy

Contents

Acknowledgments

One student I interviewed summed up his business school education by calling it a "group experience." While working on this book, I learned how right he was. Not only does the admissions process require the interaction of many different people before it concludes with acceptance or rejection; but in order to get the most from it, and later from the business-school curriculum, students must be prepared to work actively with their professors and fellow classmates.

Doing the research for this book was definitely a kind of group experience for me. I called on the knowledge, time, and support of a great many people. I want to thank my parents, Richard and Betty, who supported me all the way through Princeton and the earlier chapters of my life. I also thank my brother Richard for always asking more questions about my work. To my agent, Susan Zeckendorf, I offer special thanks; she has been with me from the beginning.

I would like to express my sincere gratitude to the following people for taking the time to talk to me about business school: Elizabeth Nill of Harvard Business School, Dave Ewing of Pace Business School, Dr. Donald G. Hester of SUNY Albany Business School, Nancy Rikoon, Gary Podorowsky, Jeremy Cohen, Leslie Fagenson, Young Suk Chi, Lawrence Hamdan, Adam Gottlieb, Sharon Tannenhauser, Thomas Ruddy, Juli Robbins, Judy Schwartz, and Ted Higgins.

Last, I'd like to thank my editors, Barbara Alpert and Jonathan Skipp, who waited those extra days for the final manuscript.

Introduction

Do You Really Want
an M.B.A.?

Do you want to be earning $200,000 a year by the time you are thirty? Do you want to start your own business, and then merge with a major corporation within the next ten years? Are you bored with your present career and would you like an opportunity to get on the fast track to wealth and success?

It would be nice to tell you that earning a Master's degree in Business Administration would bring you all of these things, but that would be a lie. An M.B.A. can do a great deal for your career, but it cannot promise to turn your life around or swell your bank account beyond your wildest dreams.

What an M.B.A. degree *can* do for you is to train you for some of the most challenging employment opportunities in business, increase your earning potential, and teach you to manage yourself and others in a way that benefits the corporation or business that employs you. That may seem like a lot to receive from a two-year professional education. But you should realize that, unlike many undergraduate degrees, an M.B.A. course goes beyond theoretical teaching. It attempts to teach the student how businesses function in the real world. And while some business schools offer more theory than others, almost all of them train their students to move directly into the work force with superior management skills.

Now that you know some of what an M.B.A. can do for a student, ask yourself if you want the degree for the right reasons. Make sure that you're not choosing business school just because your friends are going, or because you don't know what else to do with your time. It's easy to look at business school as a two-year postponement to facing the real world. Many students see it as a way to put off making their career decisions. If you are one of these people, you're making a mistake. You do not have to go to business school right away. Many students work for a few years before they apply to graduate business school. Some make career changes in their mid-thirties and decide then to get an M.B.A. Others maintain full-time work schedules and attend business school in the evenings, or on weekends.

Unlike medical schools, most M.B.A. programs are very flexible. There are many part-time programs that allow you to take only a few courses at a time while you continue with your current career or family commitments.

Your Ticket to Business School will teach you more than just how to succeed in the application process. It will show you what to expect in business school, and what you can do to survive the classroom and exam-time challenges. In addition to discussing which college courses and activities will both impress the admissions officers and aid you in your business career, this comprehensive guide will help you choose between different M.B.A. programs and show you how to present a winning application. From offering advice on Graduate Management Admission Test (GMAT) strategies to tips on collecting the best possible recommendation letters, this book will try to make the application process much more enjoyable.

Because work experience is an important component in many applications, there is information for the applicant who is considering working first, and for the one who has already been out in the "real world" for several years. Along with suggestions on finding financial aid and what to do after acceptance or rejection, there is a complete list of addresses for more than 450 business schools.

The interviews with admissions officers and business-school students will show you how the admission process really works, how to prepare for class, and what actually happens during the two years of business school. There is also advice on job-hunting and the kinds of employment opportunities for the M.B.A. graduate. A very special chapter of this book is the "Get-Into-Business-School Calendar," which will help you organize everything that needs to be done during the application process.

Ten Myths (and Ten Facts) About Business School Admissions

When you start the application process for business school, you will find that everyone is an expert. Your brother, roommate, next door neighbor, and great-aunt will all swear they know the secret to gaining admission to the best schools. No matter what they do for a living, these "friends" will feel obligated to pass on advice that they insist is absolutely foolproof. Beware of *any* information that doesn't come from those who are directly involved or were previously involved in business-school education or its admissions process. Rumors can cause you to act foolishly, so use some common sense when your cousin Harry tells you what to say on your applications or in your essays—check with your pre-business adviser or some other qualified person.

Some of the most popular rumors surrounding the business school application process are listed below. Along with these ten myths are the ten corresponding facts that bear the closest resemblance to the truth. Once you understand how the process of applying and selecting really works, you will be able to create a winning application.

MYTH #1: *Students who want to be accepted by a good business school should always work for at least two years after they graduate from college.*

FACT: While there are some schools which prefer to accept students who have first spent time in the work force, there are many other business schools that gladly accept students directly out of college. It is entirely logical for some schools to insist that their applicants pursue full-time work experience first, and many more are doing it. But many programs accept a majority of students who have only had classroom training. The reason this myth is so widespread is that many of the most prestigious business schools (like Harvard and Stanford) are famous for their policy of accepting primarily those students who have worked for at least two years after graduating from college.

If you want to continue directly into business school after receiving your college degree, then do so. Don't feel that you must interrupt your education with a job in order to be accepted by a school. And also don't feel that the top schools won't accept you without work experience. Top schools like Columbia, University of Chicago, and many others are well-known to accept students directly out of college. (For more information, see Strategy #4.)

MYTH #2: *Whether or not you like math or economics, it is almost a requirement that you major in one of them if you want to get an M.B.A.*

FACT: Unfortunately, too many students hear this myth during their early years in college and thus may select a major on that basis, simply because they believe it will please the admission officers. Simply put, business schools generally don't care what you concentrated on while in college. Although math and economics might seem "business-y" to you or your friends, you should realize that art history majors, chemistry majors, English majors, and many others have found no problem getting into or staying in some of the most selective business schools.

While it can be helpful to take certain economics and math courses, don't feel that you must concentrate in those areas. Choose a major that you will enjoy and perform well in throughout your college years. (For more information, see Strategy #2.)

MYTH #3: *Many applications for business school do not ask you to write an essay because admissions essays are used only to assess your creativity, and to business people, creativity is a liability.*

FACT: Not true. Essays are almost always requested on a business school's application. As a matter of fact, many schools ask for at least three, and some ask for as many as nine or ten. The admissions officers want to know as much about you as any close personal acquaintance might. They want to learn about your motivation, your ambition, your attitude, as well as your career plans. Because of the increased competition for spaces in business schools in recent years, you should make every effort to show the schools why you are special. They are giving you the opportunity, so use it.

Another point that should be made is that business schools are indeed looking for students with creative minds. Business leaders are only successful when they are innovative and open to new methods. The essay is your chance to display that necessary creativity. (For more information, see Strategy #8.)

MYTH #4: *Even if you may need financial aid from a school, it's better not to apply for it because making the request is the fastest way to invite a rejection letter.*

FACT: Believing this myth can be one of the biggest mistakes you ever make. If you need financial help but are reluctant to apply for it because a classmate tells you that financial aid requests to an overburdened school will elicit quick rejections, think again. While it might seem logical to you that a school would rather not give scholarships if they can accept enough students who can pay their own way, that's not the way it works. If a school says (and it usually does) that it uses need-blind admissions, or that acceptance has nothing to do with your financial status, believe it.

If you do not apply for aid and later get accepted, it will be too late to ask the school for a scholarship. Grant and loan deadlines arrive very early during the application process, so don't plan to apply later on. What good is an acceptance letter if you won't be able to afford to attend the school? (For more information, see Strategy #14.)

MYTH #5: *If you have been in the work force for several years and now have decided to apply to business school, you probably don't need to study for the Graduate Management Admission Test (GMAT) like the applicants who lack your business experience.*

FACT: No matter how many years you've been in the business world and no matter how high an executive position you've achieved, you will not score well on the GMAT unless you study for it. Some people believe that this exam measures your business knowledge or aptitude. It is not until they get fifteen minutes into the test that they realize they are being asked to solve algebra and geometry problems. Business experience is not going to get you through this exam. While it may help you in other phases of the application process, it will not give you an advantage on the GMAT. No one is at an advantage unless he or she prepares for it. (For more information, see Strategy #7.)

MYTH #6: *The way to choose the right business school is to find out whose graduates receive the highest salary offers upon graduation.*

FACT: Although many students do consider earning potential when weighing one school against another, you should not over-look the many other differences between the various business schools. Not only do the schools follow different teaching methods, but they also offer different concentrations. If you know what field you want to enter, you should be certain that all of the schools to which you apply offer a concentration in that area.

Along with the curriculum, you'll also want to consider the location, size, cost, and many other aspects of a business school. (For more information, see Strategy #5.)

MYTH #7: *Business schools care more about your entrepreneurial activities than they do about the courses you took or the grades you received in college.*

FACT: Rarely will you be able to get into a business school solely on the basis of your extracurricular activities. Unless you founded a million-dollar business during your freshman year and increased your staff to more than a hundred, it will be almost impossible to convince the admissions office that it should disregard your transcripts. Although business schools provide you with professional skills, they are still educational institutions—and, therefore, concerned with your academic records. Impressive entrepreneurial activities will make your application stand out, but cannot substitute for advanced courses and good grades. (For more information, see Strategy #3.)

MYTH #8: *Although there are many different business schools in this country, you should only consider attending those in the "top ten." Otherwise, it will be difficult to find a good job.*

FACT: Of course it is easier to find a job if you earn a degree from one of the ten best schools in the country, but who's to say you're going to face an unusually difficult job hunt if you attend a less prestigious school? You will always hear the term *top ten*—top ten schools, top ten firms, top ten corporations, top ten cities, and so on. What should be important to you is not just rank, but the school's curriculum, facilities, teaching quality, and placement records.

There is no official list of the top ten business schools, but it should be clear to you that those ten business schools can't be the only ones whose graduating students find good jobs. (For more information, see Strategy #5.)

MYTH #9: *Letters of recommendation and contacts have little to do with the admissions process for business school.*

FACT: Most business schools do not grant admissions interviews to their applicants. Unlike college admission officers, the business school admissions people cannot learn about your personal qualities during a thirty-minute interview—they must rely on what others say about you in a written recommendation. Because of this, it cannot be stressed enough that good letters can, and will, make all the difference in the world when your file is being considered.

A contact who is a wealthy and powerful alumnus or important faculty member can sometimes be even more important to your admissions prospects than your letters of recommendation. Never hesitate to contact someone who can improve your chances for admission. (For more information, see Strategy #9.)

MYTH #10: *If you decide to work before pursuing an M.B.A., it does not matter to the business schools what kind of job you have. Any job will provide good business experience.*

FACT: Don't kid yourself. If you are working for the sole reason of developing a good resume for your business-school application, it matters a great deal where you find employment. In order to improve your chances for admission, it makes sense to work at a job that involves some form of management. Even if you don't have people working under you, your position should be one that gives you some responsibility and contact with people. On the other hand, if you've been working in a nonrelated job, and then suddenly decide to apply to business school, you should explain on your application what led you to apply for a graduate business program. (For more information, see Strategy #4.)

Taking the Right
College Curriculum

If you are fortunate, your college may provide you with a
pre-business adviser. This person is usually a dean or professor
who can counsel you on your preparation for business school. If
there is no person in the dean's office with this title, then check
with the university's career placement center. If there is no one
to offer advice on a good pre-business curriculum, you can rely
on the information provided in this chapter.

You should disregard all rumors that hinted that you should
major in economics or math in order to get into a top business
school. There are no required college courses for business school.
But while there are no courses you *must* take, there are certain
courses and major areas of study that may help prepare you or
put you at an advantage once you arrive at school.

The two years you will spend working toward an M.B.A.
degree require you to utilize a number of important skills. Many
of these skills can be learned while you're still in college.

In the past, many of the students who pursued M.B.A. degrees were business or economics majors in college. Today,
students major in many areas: architecture, romance languages,
political science, engineering, music, chemistry, and other
disciplines. While some majors might better prepare you for
business school courses, there is no particular concentration
that is certain to improve your chances for admission. A strong
liberal arts education, and a major in a field that particularly
interests you, is the best preparation for the specialized training
you will get in business school.

Here is an example of a student whose concern about getting into graduate school persuaded her to make a poor choice of major.

From her first days in college, Beatrice knew that she would someday want to get an M.B.A. degree. She was very much interested in entering advertising, and she was sure an M.B.A. would put her onto the fast track to success. Her first concern then was to design a curriculum which would be sure to impress the business-school admissions people. For the first two semesters of college, Beatrice took courses in political science, English, math, history, biology, music, and art history.

When sophomore year began, her academic adviser asked Beatrice which courses she had enjoyed most. She answered, "English and biology." When asked which courses she had disliked, she answered, "Math." She had only taken the course because her school required it of all freshman students. Still, when it came time to declare her major, Beatrice chose math. She had convinced herself that the best way to show the "right stuff" for business school was to choose a "businesslike" concentration like math.

Too many students like Beatrice make the mistake of majoring in a discipline they dislike. They agree to suffer through agonizing years of math or computer science just to prove they have minds for business. But Beatrice's suffering didn't end with her courses. On top of not enjoying her courses, she scored very badly on her exams. She had been a mediocre student in the subject, and as the concepts grew more complex, her grades plummeted. Her C-plus average doomed her business school applications. The admissions people looked at her grades in her math courses and wondered what on earth had made her concentrate in an area where she got a C-plus average, especially when she had gotten A's and B's in her other courses? Her hopes were dashed—she did *not* impress the admissions people by majoring in math.

A business school may prefer that you choose a business-oriented major (if there is such a thing), but they'd be much happier to see a transcript with a major course-load of high grades. Even though a mathematics background might prove beneficial in Beatrice's business-school education, her transcript full of low grades is a liability. Although there are no majors that will improve your chances for admission, there are a few majors that offer an excellent background for graduate school and your business career. In addition to mathematics, you might consider accounting, economics, statistics, English, and computer science.

Like math, accounting, economics and statistics will teach the pre-business student to work with figures and financial formulas. Although some students enter business school without having cracked a math or economics book since high school or freshman year of college, most realize that their success in business school hinges on their ability and willingness to, as the jargon puts it, crunch (work with) numbers. In addition, many business schools require entering students to demonstrate their math proficiency by taking a math placement exam or by registering for a short math-review course.

Because of the widespread use of computers in corporations and in business schools (some schools even include the price of a personal computer in each student's tuition bill), it is important to understand not only how computers work, but their applications for business. Computer literacy is an important skill for the pre-business student to develop in college.

Finally, English, with an emphasis on writing, can be a useful major area of study. Good writing skills are vitally important in the business world. You don't want to be one of the M.B.A. graduates who shudders at the thought of writing a business report for a client or putting your thoughts in a memo to a manager in your own firm.

Liberal Arts Versus Science/Engineering

Whether you attend a liberal arts college or an engineering school is unimportant to most admissions officers. Neither will give you a better shot at admittance to business school; you must persuade them that your college major, combined with a graduate degree, will prepare you for the business career you seek.

Many business-school classes will consist of approximately twenty percent science and engineering majors and about eighty percent majors from the social sciences, humanities, and other areas.

In recent years, more engineering students have sought M.B.A.s in the area of computers and information services—a specialty that many engineering firms find valuable.

Courses That Teach Good Business Skills

Although most business schools offer a wide variety of concentrations, you will probably not be allowed to focus on an area until you have completed the core curriculum. Most schools have a core curriculum of at least seven or eight different courses, so it's a good idea to prepare yourself for them while you're still in college. One college course that will help prepare you for the first year of business school is calculus. While you may not need to use calculus in all your business classes, you will find it helpful in many of them.

Students who are already in business school comment that a background in calculus will give the incoming student a psychological boost. Arriving at business school without having taken calculus means that you already have a handicap. Even a summer calculus course at a community college can help boost your confidence.

Another useful college course is one in corporate finance, a class which is usually offered by the economics department. This course will introduce you to such corporate concerns as annual reports, investment policies, and other basic issues and concepts. In many colleges, this course will utilize actual business cases—just as the business schools do. This is one way to learn how the case-study method works before you begin your M.B.A. program.

You may also want to study macroeconomics. Learning the

basics of monetary systems and world economic activity will introduce you to many of the terms and tools you'll need during your first year at business school.

Graded Versus Pass/Fail Courses

When selecting your college courses each semester, keep in mind that the business schools will be primarily concerned with the grades that you get in those courses. Even if your college allows you to take as many pass/fail courses as you like, admissions officers are not going to look kindly on a transcript full of P grades. The business school has to rank its candidates, and it needs to know if your passing grade was an A-plus or a C-minus.

One good rule is to utilize the pass/fail option as infrequently as possible. If your college requires that you take thirty-two courses during your four years, it might be wise to limit yourself to no more than four pass/fail courses—and if you're applying to the very best business schools, just two or three.

Sometimes students find themselves panicking in the face of a very important course, and quickly change the grading option to pass/fail, only to find out later that they received an A on the final exam. If this happens to you, and you really would like to let the business schools know what your letter grade *would* have been, you might ask your professor to write a note explaining the situation. Some admissions officers will take this into consideration when they judge your file.

Activities That Will Strengthen Your Application

Business schools are perhaps more interested in your extracurricular activities than any other type of graduate school. In addition to your grades, GMAT scores, and work experience, your activities and hobbies will play an important part in your application. Of course it matters that you've taken all the right courses and received good grades, but you can demonstrate your versatility by showing the admissions office a high level of involvement in different activities.

It would be much simpler for the admissions people to accept applicants solely on the basis of their grade point average, so why do they bother asking for so much more information? Why do they care how you spend your time? If you have a high class-rank, what difference does it make to them if you don't participate in any clubs or activities? The simple answer is that the admissions people are looking for students who will most likely contribute to their respective business schools, and who will most likely succeed in a business career. Grades and scores alone are not enough to predict your future.

While this does not mean you should run off and sign up for a dozen college or off-campus activities simply because you want to fill all the spaces on your business school application, you should be aware that students with high grades and test scores have been rejected because they had no activities or outside interests to discuss in their essays and applications. While you can't get into a good business school on the strength of your activities alone, there's almost no way to assemble a strong application without them.

The best way to look at an activity is as an extension of your personality. Not only will it help you develop certain qualities or skills, but it will also give you the opportunity to demonstrate a talent while it is being perfected. And talent—*any* talent—is what catches the attention of an admissions officer.

Before you sign up for too many groups or clubs, realize that more is not necessarily better. It's not the number of activities that is important, it's your level of involvement with the activities. Probably the best rule is to sign up for those activities that truly interest you. Whether it's the newspaper, the student government, or the baseball team, you should choose it because you enjoy it. Since your membership in a college activity may last as long as four years, it's a waste of time and energy to join something that you dislike.

As you meet other pre-business students, you will find that they generally fall into three categories: those who participate in all the hard-core business activities, those who sign up for one or two significant activities that teach useful management skills, and those who pursue no activities whatsoever. We've already established that to be part of the third group is a mistake, so let's examine the first two groups.

During his sophomore year, Eddie decided that he wanted to pursue a career in business. A hardworking and ambitious student, he decided to build up a long list of business-oriented activities on his resume. The first thing he did was to run for treasurer of the student government. He knew it would give him the opportunity to work with money and demonstrate his management skills. Although students may not realize it, student government positions are not only attractive to the pre-law student, but because they require management ability, they can also prove helpful to the pre-business student.

Another sophomore, Celia, chose a less obvious pre-business activity. Many of her friends suggested she look for a position as financial manager of some organization, but instead Celia chose to found and direct a drama group on campus. Why did she do it when she knew she wanted to go to business school? Because she wanted to do what she enjoyed and because she knew that her position with the group would provide her with some important management skills. In order to start a drama group, Celia first had to raise money. She then had to publicize the activity, select members, and organize and direct them.

How many more duties does a full-time business person have than the ones that Celia had to concern herself with while running her new dramatic group? Although it was certainly not an obvious choice for a business student, the drama group was something that she liked doing, as well as something that gave her an unusual kind of leadership experience.

Remember, if you join a club or activity that you don't enjoy, you will probably never achieve a position of responsibility in the group. If you don't earn such positions in your activities, the business schools may assume that you spent very little time on them; and if the admissions people believe that you spent little time on your activities, your application will be just as lackluster as that of a student who joined no clubs or activities.

Another suggestion is that you should try to focus on just two or three major activities in the beginning of your undergraduate career, then later choose the one to which you would like to devote the most time. If you choose more than one or two, you won't have sufficient time to do well in your classwork.

Fund Drives

Hector decided early to find an activity that would allow him to demonstrate business experience. As a freshman, he heard that there was an annual campus fund drive whose goal was to raise $30,000. Being director of the drive would have been an ideal position, but since he had no experience in fund-raising, Hector knew it would be a catastrophe if he tried to take on such a huge challenge so early in his college career.

Hector decided that the best way to learn about fund-raising was to start small and apply for another position on the fund drive. After a director was selected, Hector asked the student if he could be his special assistant and serve as a "gopher." While it might seem demeaning to some students, offering to work as an "I'll-do-anything-you-want-me-to-do" is a good way to learn all the phases of organizing and running a successful organization. By the end of the drive, Hector had served temporarily as office manager, typist, publicist, and treasurer. Although he held no formal title, Hector had put himself in a position to take on any job that needed to be done. He also got to meet some of the more influential faculty members when he accompanied the director to important meetings.

By the time sophomore year arrived, Hector felt secure enough to apply for the position as director of the campus fund drive. Although a senior had generally held the position in the past, his extensive involvement as a freshman gave him the experience necessary to take on the job. Later, when he needed business school references, he was able to ask several top faculty members to write recommendation letters on his behalf which described how much he had achieved as a fund-raiser.

Radio Station

Are you wondering how working at the radio station can help a pre-business student? To begin with, there is the job of business manager. Wherever your school station gets its financial backing, it certainly needs someone to pay its bills and to keep track of its bank statements and income. Some campus radio stations pay their student workers, so the business manager will handle that, too.

Another position open to students is as the radio station's advertising director. Whether local, national, or public-service, advertising is an important function in every station. Susan set her mind to becoming advertising director of her school's music station. Starting from the bottom, she volunteered to take on a district of stores that had not been buying time on the station. Susan managed to bring in some new ad revenue and attracted the attention of senior staff members. Within five months, she was promoted to assistant advertising director and given the responsibility of directing a small staff to focus on developing new accounts.

By the end of her junior year, Susan had learned a lot about the business side of running a radio station, and she had acquired knowledge of management by directing her own small staff. When she applied to business school, she was able to describe her skills in sales as well as in personal motivation. In order to bring her involvement a little more to life, Susan made a fifteen-minute taped sales presentation to send to each school. The cassette allowed the admissions people to hear her professionalism and special skills in action.

School Newspaper

The positions of business manager and advertising director are also available on a campus daily or weekly newspaper. One advantage to performing this job on a publication is that your work appears on paper and your name is in print. How many people know the name of the radio station's advertising director? Not many, probably. While you may think it vain to want to see your name in print, it can be especially gratifying, when applying to schools, to send a sample copy of the paper and let the admissions people see your work in black-and-white.

Another business-related position at the newspaper is circulation manager. Although not very glamorous, this job can teach you to motivate others and to take responsibility for getting the paper to its readership.

Fraternities, Sororities, Social Groups

If you belong to some sort of social group and would like to take on some duty that relates to business, you might offer to act as treasurer for several semesters. You don't have to be a math or accounting major in order to take over this duty. If you know how to balance a bank book and budget money wisely over long periods of time, you should do well.

Pre-Business Society and Speakers' Bureau

A good way to follow up on your interest in business and management is to organize a pre-business society. Most schools don't have one, so you can help decide what might interest students fascinated by the corporate world. Maybe you could begin a speakers' program that invites business people to address students on campus.

Jeff was a junior majoring in French literature. When he considered that his record might look too unfocused to the business-school admissions people, he decided to create an activity that would suit his needs and display his interest in the business field. He did this by organizing a group of twenty students and getting himself selected president of the "Pre-Business Lecture Society." The next thing Jeff did was to visit the school's alumni office. He had a plan to invite a different person to campus every other week to talk about subjects like entrepreneurism, job-hunting, business school, investment banking, advertising, and so on. He started by selecting his first speakers from a list of active alumni who were knowledgeable in those areas.

The new organization was a big hit on campus. Not only did Jeff's programs attract over a hundred students for each lecture, but he even had some alumni calling to offer their services to speak about their professions. Although the lectures were free to students during the first three months, Jeff then decided that he could charge a small entrance fee. By raising money to offer a small honorarium, Jeff was able to invite nonalumni lecturers to the university.

The benefits of organizing such a program were numerous. Not only did Jeff impress the admissions people when he applied to graduate school, but he was also able to learn more about the various professions available to him once he graduated. Finally, Jeff managed to make some valuable early contacts with people he might never have met until after graduation. In order to describe the program he designed to business schools when he applied, Jeff sent a description of the project and a list of all his past speakers and the companies for which they worked.

Political and Civic Groups

Even if you have not been politically active or particularly civic minded, there are positions that you can fill or even create if you want more business-related experience. One such job is that of publicist. Every organization that wants to attract members or guests for special events needs someone to coordinate publicity for them. A publicist will usually be given a specified budget and told to use the money in the best possible way so that each dollar spent attracts a certain number of people. This position requires that you use creativity, as well as business skills, in figuring out how to get the most for your employer's money.

This position is similar to that of an advertising accounts manager. When a corporate client hires an advertising agency to handle his account, he tells the advertiser that he will give him X amount of money, hoping to attract Y amount of new business. Of course you'll be working on a smaller scale with mimeographed fliers, newspaper ads, and so on, but the concept is essentially the same.

Athletic Activities

Although there is no direct connection between sports and business school, many athletes do apply for admission. A warning to student-athletes: if your grades and scores are low, belonging to a sports team is probably one of the activities that will mean the least to the admissions people. Put simply, athletic activities cannot make up for low grades as substantially as being advertising director for the campus daily. Aside from that, there are many benefits that can arise from participating in a sport. What an athlete might want to emphasize in his application are the things that he has learned as a team-competitor on the playing field, as well as the things he has learned as a solo competitor in the classroom.

In addition to these activities, you may also choose to join such other business-oriented groups as the economics society or investment club (if they are available at your school).

The suggestions offered above are just that: ideas you may or may not choose to pursue. Any college activity that matters to you can be put to good use when you write your essays for business school applications, as long as you describe how your participation has contributed to your growth as an individual, how you've changed as a result of your involvement, and why you chose to do it in the first place. A successful business executive is a man or woman of many talents, and developing your best abilities is one of the most important parts of your college education.

Time Off Before Applying

This chapter is directed specifically at those people who take time off before applying to business school. Whether you've been out of college for more than five years or you're graduating now and are planning to work for a few years before graduate school, this strategy can tell you how to plan your career as an M.B.A.

When You've Been Out of College for a Few Years

Students have many different reasons for wanting to get an M.B.A. after they've been out of academia for a few years. Some decide to return for the degree because they feel it will help them earn a promotion in their jobs. Others are making career changes and need the M.B.A. to qualify for a new position. Still others attend business school later because they couldn't afford it right after college. Let's look at what happened to Mary when she decided to return to school six years after her college graduation.

Mary had gotten married three months after graduating from college. At the time, she and her husband decided that they wanted to have children very early in their marriage. Two years after they were married, Mary gave birth to a baby boy. After four more years passed and her son was in nursery school, Mary decided that she wanted to go back to work. After interviewing for several months, however, she found that her bachelor's degree in philosophy wasn't attracting any offers. Her husband suggested that she attend law school, but Mary felt the three-year commitment would be too great. Knowing she could get an M.B.A. in two years, she decided on business school.

Since she had a young child, Mary needed to attend a business school within commuting distance from her home. After sending away for catalogs from some of the nearby schools, Mary wrote to her old college and asked for a copy of her transcript. With the transcript in hand, Mary made appointments with deans at each of the MBA programs that interested her. They spoke with her and described what their programs offered. She found that there were full-time as well as part-time programs. She could even take summer courses, which would make her work load a little lighter during the fall and spring semesters.

When she was ready to apply, Mary took a review course before registering for the Graduate Management Admission Test (GMAT), and filled out her applications. Her biggest concern was her letters of recommendation. Since she had been out of college for six years, she doubted that her former professors remembered her well. But the deans at some of the business schools told her that the admissions office would gladly accept letters from nonacademic people. Since Mary had volunteered at the local YWCA, she asked the director to evaluate her work and to send a letter to the schools. She also asked one of her co-workers on the school PTA to write a recommendation.

In her applications, Mary made sure to discuss what she wanted to do with her M.B.A., as well as commenting on her family life now that she was a mother. Because the populations of many business schools have a median age of twenty-nine or above, it is vital that each applicant write about his or her life experiences *outside* of school. They are an important part of what makes you a potential success in business, and will help the admissions officers understand you better as a person.

If You Want to Wait Before Applying to Business School

Perhaps you are graduating from college and don't want to apply to business schools yet. Are there any special problems to be aware of? Are there disadvantages to doing this?

You will find that there are many different ways to pursue a business-school education. You could apply to school and get accepted, then ask for a two-year deferral so that you can work. But if you know you don't want to be in school right now, it may be wise to wait. Though some schools will accept you and allow you to postpone your first semester for a year or two, many business schools require accepted students to begin the very next September.

If you're certain that you want to work first, before you apply, there are several things you should do. First, visit your professors and deans before you leave the campus at the end of senior year. Tell them that you are considering applying to graduate business programs in the near future, and ask if they would write a general letter of recommendation that speaks to your integrity, commitment, and potential as an M.B.A. student. Don't have them address the letter to a particular school, even if you have some idea where you might apply. They may simply use the salutation: "To the Admissions Committee."

Once the letters are written, have them forward the originals to the career placement office or dean's office, where they can be placed in your files for the future. Check with the dean and find out how long such letters will remain on file. Because of limited space, they may only allow them to remain for four or five years. For a small fee, you can probably renew the file every three years thereafter. Once you've decided to apply, you can merely contact your college and supply them with the addresses of the business schools so that they can forward your letters accordingly.

As far as the GMAT is concerned, it is up to you as to when you take it. If you have studied math during the past two years and are afraid that you will have forgotten the concepts in another year or two, you should probably take the exam now. If, on the other hand, you feel you will need a lot of time to review for it, you can decide to register for it later.

What to Do with Your Time Before Business School

There are many things you may want to do before returning to get your M.B.A. You may decide to raise a family, travel, or even study for another graduate degree. But the most common activity for pre-M.B.A. students is to take on a full-time job. If this is what you decide, it's a good idea to look for work in the field that you plan to pursue *after* you get your M.B.A. If you can plan carefully, you might be able to convince your company to pay the costs of your degree. Of course you'd be obligated to return to the job, but the money you'd save could certainly make it worthwhile.

One Harvard graduate who is now working for a consulting firm explained that he decided not to go directly to business school because he was simply tired of the lecture-studying-homework routine. He accepted a position at a firm that will reimburse him for the cost of his M.B.A. program if he agrees to return to the company after receiving his degree.

Another reason many students take time off before business school is that they have won fellowships. Any fellowship that awards you the opportunity to study or travel abroad is truly worthwhile, so take advantage of it *before* you begin business school. You may never again be able to take the time off once you begin a full-time business career.

Deciding Where to Apply

As mentioned earlier, a popular myth about business school is that an applicant must attend one of the top ten schools to find a good job after graduation. Not only is it foolish to believe this myth, but students should realize that there are so many factors to consider when selecting a school that focusing solely on prestige is a bad idea. Each school is different, and many offer advantages not available at others. What is most important for each applicant is to determine what you want to gain from a particular school. This strategy will help you make those decisions.

Since you may have only heard about such big-name business schools as Harvard or Stanford, or only about the ones in your community, it's a good idea to do some research and familiarize yourself with the many schools not in your area. In the appendix of this book, there is a comprehensive list of business schools and their addresses, so you can send away for brochures and catalogs. If your college or a nearby university has a counseling office on campus, it will usually have a complete collection of catalogs.

It is also helpful to study *The Official Guide to MBA Programs*, produced by the Graduate Management Admission Council. This is the only official directory and provides information on all the different business schools. The extensive listings include recommended GMAT scores and grade point averages for applicants to each of the schools. If you can't find it at a nearby bookstore, borrow a copy from your library or counseling center.

Once you have glanced through the directory and some catalogs, make a list of approximately twenty-five schools that interest you and then check them against the information that follows.

Your Grades and GMAT Scores

Whenever you read about recommended grade averages and GMAT scores for particular schools, remember that these numbers are usually mean figures. In other words, you are being given a sort of midpoint to use to guide your own chances for admission. Many business schools list the recommended grades and scores in their separate catalogs, but some are reluctant to give you any guide whatsoever. These grades and scores are never exact, so a school that lists a B-plus will generally accept a certain number of B and B-minus students, just as it will accept a certain number of A-minus and A students.

While you should use your grades and GMAT scores as a guide to select most of the schools in your pool of applications, don't be afraid also to apply to those that are listed as being above your range. You may have some other notable strength in your application: an unusual job experience, or geographical diversity, which might outweigh a disappointing GMAT score or middling grade point average.

As you read the other factors that follow, think about which schools satisfy your concerns. You will probably decide to apply to nine or ten schools, so only eliminate those schools that really don't fulfill your needs. Be realistic in your evaluation; it's easy to become too picky and to eliminate schools simply because they aren't perfect in every way.

Curriculum

Every business school does not offer the same courses. Some programs are extremely narrow, while others are very comprehensive. While first year students in different schools may take similar courses (in Finance, Marketing, Operations Management, Accounting, Organizational Behavior, Information Systems, and so on), second year students most often take electives in order to concentrate in a specific area. It's a good idea to look over the course offerings in the catalogs in order to evaluate each school. If you plan a career in International Finance, it's important to choose a school with plenty of courses in that area.

Something that is becoming increasingly popular at many business schools is the opportunity to study for a combined degree. Perhaps you would like to receive a law degree as well as a business degree. There are also programs that allow you to combine engineering with an M.B.A. One reason these combined degree programs are attractive is that they provide you with the opportunity to complete both degrees in less time than is usually required to attend each school separately. They also prepare you for special opportunities in your area of interest. After completing a combined M.B.A./law degree program, you would be uniquely well qualified to practice law in one of the top corporate firms, or serve as legal counsel for a major corporation.

A last note about curriculum: if you have no idea what area of specialty you will pursue, you may be better off choosing a large school with many options open to you when you make that decision.

Method of Teaching

An interesting aspect of business schools is that they do not employ one particular form of teaching. You may have heard the term *case method*. This is a popular form of training students by utilizing studies of actual business situations faced by real corporations. Harvard Business School tries to teach all of its classes in this manner, believing both that it is more practical and that it best teaches the students how the real world works.

There are also schools that only rarely use the case method. These are heavily theoretical schools which rely more on textbook study. There are also schools that emphasize the "numbers" side of business training, and others that focus more on managing people. MIT is one school which places heavy emphasis on mathematics in its courses. Read the catalog to learn about a particular school's method of teaching.

Prestige of the School

Too many students may allow a school's prestige to become their sole motivation in applying for its M.B.A. program. While there is no formal list of prestige schools, the elite top fifteen or so usually includes Harvard, Stanford, Wharton at University of Pennsylvania, University of Chicago, Dartmouth's Amos Tuck Business School, Northwestern, Columbia, and several others. When considering your application to one of the best-known schools, never allow the undergraduate school's reputation to influence your decision. For instance, Yale's M.B.A. program is generally not as highly rated as the Yale University name overall. Just because a school's undergraduate program or its law school is well respected, it doesn't mean that the business school is always of the same quality.

Remember too that there are many other fine schools that can suit your needs. While these elite business schools offer a terrific opportunity to the best-qualified applicants, if you haven't got high grades, top scores, a winning resume of activities, and a great collection of recommendations, you will probably be wasting your application fee. But, like any worthwhile goal, admittance to these schools is worth trying for. In addition to having established and respected names, these programs offer superb instruction, a comprehensive curriculum, and some of the best records of placing graduates in jobs in the finest corporations in the world.

Quality of Facilities

Another consideration should be the quality of the school's facilities. This applies to the library as well as to the career placement office and available housing. The best way to investigate these three facilities is either by writing to the library, the housing office, and the career placement office and asking for literature, or, even better, by visiting the campus and seeing the facilities first-hand.

No matter how great a school's reputation is, the facilities that it offers are very important. If on-campus living space is very limited, you may be forced to live off campus and commute from a distance. The placement office is vitally important, too; it is your connection to the real world's employment opportunities. If it does not attract a large number of corporate recruiters, then your employment search will be noticeably more difficult.

Quality of Faculty

You may never be taught by a Nobel Prize winner in economics, even if there is one on the faculty. You should simply be concerned that there are plenty of instructors who have their doctorates in their particular specialties. Avoid any school that allows fellow graduate students to teach significant core courses.

Location of the School

A school's location can be another prime factor in your application decisions. Location involves both the school's setting and its distance from your home.

If you grew up in a rural setting and attended a college out in the country, you might find it difficult to attend a school in the center of a major city. Since there are more than 450 business programs available to you, you are not limited to one type of environment.

For those students who are accustomed to city life, it might be difficult adjusting to a rural campus. You may want the entertainment that bars, movie houses, and clubs in a large city will offer. Another advantage to attending a school in a major city is that there tend to be many more job opportunities. More recruiters are likely to visit your school if you are only a few minutes from their offices.

Students considering a school's location usually have two principal concerns. They are often worried about the costs of traveling cross country to a school, and about the wisdom of attending a school in a state where they do not intend to work after graduation. The first point can be important because shipping your furnishings and books back and forth can be costly. Add to that your long distance phone bills and you'll see how expensive it can be to attend a school a long way from home.

If you're wondering about going to school in a state where you may never work, don't. Just because you plan to work on the West Coast but you want to attend school in the East doesn't mean that you won't get to interview with West Coast-based companies. Not only will many businesses send representatives to your campus, but you can also write to them. If they like your resume, they may fly you out for an interview—at their expense!

Tuition and Other Costs

The cost of a particular program may influence your decision to apply. Business-school costs range from surprisingly inexpensive to practically prohibitive. State schools may cost as little as two thousand dollars a year, while some of the big-name prestige schools charge up to fifteen thousand dollars a year.

Find out about all of your potential financial resources before eliminating the more expensive schools from your list. There are grant and loan programs that will help you pay for school.

In Strategy #14 there is information on how to find grants, loans, and private scholarships that are awarded both to students who can show need and those who cannot. Look into all the possibilities before you decide against applying to the schools of your choice.

How Many Applications

Now that you know which factors to consider when selecting a school, to how many should you actually apply? Depending on what you feel you can afford to spend, you should probably try to apply to as many as nine or ten schools. Don't skimp here. If you only apply to two or three schools, you may get rejected and have to wait a whole year to apply again. Assume that there is a lot of competition at *each* school, not just at the most prestigious schools.

Where to Get Advice

In addition to reading catalogs and brochures on the various business schools, you should collect more information by speaking with the pre-business adviser, if there is one on campus. This person can give you insights about each school, as well as supply you with statistics on the students who graduated from your college and are now attending some of the schools that interest you.

You should also try to make contact with some students who are already in business schools. Ask them for details on student life, class work, and any other topics that aren't answered by the material you've already read.

The Older Student

As we discussed earlier, business-school classes are not limited to the twenty-two-year-old students who have just graduated from college. Many schools have a student body with the median age hovering around twenty-seven or twenty-eight. So when we speak about the older student in this section, we are referring to an applicant who is above the median—someone who is thirty-one or older.

Business school is a viable option for people of various ages who are looking for new employment opportunities. Don't be concerned that you may be the only person at your business school trying to change careers after thirty-five, or that you will be the only former housewife with grown children who now wants a business career. You will find that there is no average business school student. The M.B.A. has only become popular during the past nine or ten years, so people at all levels of career growth are discovering it now.

Business School for the Older Student

If you've been reading the catalogs of many business schools, you may have realized that the schools require a full-time schedule for those who want to complete the program in two years' time. Older students, often with family responsibilities, may not be able to enjoy the same flexibility that young, single students have.

Fortunately, there are many part-time business programs for people who need to continue working full-time during the day. Many of these programs offer two two-and-a-half-hour classes each evening, Monday through Friday. Since most part-time students can fit in only two courses each semester, it usually takes close to five or six years to earn the degree. If you think this is too long, then you may consider taking classes during the summers. This can cut almost two years from that schedule. In order to find out which schools offer part-time programs, contact the schools that interest you. Make sure you specifically request information on part-time programs. The application form and catalog are sometimes different from that for the full-time program.

Some unusual options exist for part-time business students who've achieved a certain level of success in management. They may be able to arrange abbreviated working schedules with their companies in order to attend three-day weekend classes so they can complete degree requirements sooner. The business school's counseling office may be able to help you find the attendance option that best suits your life-style and needs.

Work Experience:
How It Applies

Business schools are not only interested in your school activities; they want to know what type of employment you have held both in summer and term-time. It's not hard to understand why work experience would be particularly important; like anything to which you have devoted your time, it is something that will distinguish your application from the rest. For that reason, we will review a variety of summer and on-campus jobs that can be valuable either because they are especially appealing to the business schools or because they can give you useful business skills.

Since M.B.A. programs exist in order to train managers and business people, it is absolutely essential that you begin to look at your work life as a career from the minute you get accepted to college.

Summer Jobs

Most college students work during the summer, but they do so for different reasons. They work in order to earn money; to use the employment experience to build their resumes; and so that they can begin to make career decisions or learn about a particular field. Whatever their reasons for working, students will always be asked by the business schools to explain how they spent their summers. If you spend every summer vacationing on a Greek island or lying on the beach, the admissions people may wonder if you are really serious about your career.

Sally, a pre-business student, made good use of her summer vacations, knowing that she would eventually have a resume with a long list of interesting jobs. During her freshman year in college, Sally decided that she liked the idea of publishing as a career. Although some of her classmates commented that publishing salaries were generally lower than those in other fields, Sally decided that it was a business too fascinating to overlook simply because her earning potential might be limited. In December of her freshman year, Sally visited the career placement office on her campus and spoke with a counselor. During her meeting, she learned about the various career opportunities in the book-publishing business.

Sally found that there were many other opportunities in the field beside that of becoming an editor. Since she was interested in the business end of publishing, she set her ultimate goal at becoming the publisher of a major publishing house within the next fifteen years. While it is unusual for an eighteen-year-old student to make such far-reaching plans so early on, Sally is just the type of ambitious student that business schools are looking for. They encourage applicants to have specific, focused career goals. While it may actually be difficult for Sally to reach her goals in the time projected, admissions officers are satisfied to see that she has begun to plan that far ahead.

Judging that it would be next to impossible for a freshman to get a summer job at a major book publisher, Sally considered applying to smaller publishers. After doing some research, she also learned that many magazine staffs included a book editor, so she applied for intern positions at magazines too. Eventually Sally landed a job as a clerical intern for the book editor at a popular woman's magazine.

During her sophomore year, Sally planned for her next summer. She was still interested in getting into the business side of book publishing, and she would have liked to work in the part of the company that sells serializations of books to magazines and newspapers. But since Sally didn't have the book publishing experience to get this particular job, she applied for, and got, a summer internship in the editorial division of a paperback book publisher.

The following summer—the summer before business school applications had to be completed—Sally believed she could land a job working in subsidiary rights if she packaged herself properly. Along with her resume, she enclosed a carefully written cover letter detailing her experience in publishing and her observations of how serial rights were sold to magazines, a process she'd learned about while working with the book editor two summers earlier. After pitching herself in this manner, Sally was successful in obtaining a special summer internship in the rights department of a well-known New York publishing house.

Sally had chosen a career goal with a unique focus, and had directed her efforts toward gaining hands-on experience in the field of her choice. Her progress toward this goal made convincing essay material on her business school applications.

Another student followed a different path, and the results surprised him. Harold came from a middle-class family that owned and ran a successful refrigeration business. As the eldest son, Harold expected to be president of the company someday, after finishing college and business school. But in the meantime he wanted to avoid the company office and to spend his summers doing as he wished. Getting into a good business school was not high on his list of priorities, since he believed that his assured future in management would make him an obviously good candidate for an M.B.A. degree.

Harold's summers during college were a perfect example of how not to prepare for the future: he worked as a lifeguard at the local pool, went backpacking in the mountains with a couple of friends, and shared a beach house with a group of college fraternity brothers. When he finally met with his college's pre-business adviser in the early fall of his senior year, Harold was amazed to hear that his applications to Stanford and Wharton would not be encouraged because of his mediocre grades and dearth of business experience. His adviser recommended that he apply as soon as possible to the state university business school, which favored local students and would be interested in Harold because other members of his family (his uncle and cousin) were alumni.

Harold simply felt that his future was too secure for him to be concerned with finding significant employment during the summers. He felt that his ability to pay the tuition, coupled with his future position in his family's business, would be sufficient to get him admitted to a top business school. But all schools, public or private, large or small, want to see an effort on each student's part to gain business experience before beginning graduate school. And admissions officers can only measure your potential by considering your past achievements. Don't short-circuit your opportunities by forgetting this important point.

We're not saying that you shouldn't enjoy your vacations or that you should work every minute you're not in class. Just remember that work experience is an important part of the total picture when you plan to apply to graduate business school.

Term-Time Jobs

Many college students take on part-time employment, on-campus or off-campus in a neighboring community. While you may only be working ten or fifteen hours each week, the job you find can provide you with more than just a weekly paycheck. You may choose to work in the dining hall, but it could be more beneficial to pursue a position in the controller's office, the financial aid office, or the economics library, for a few possibilities. The pay scale in many schools is often determined by class (freshman, sophomore) rather than by the type of position held, so it's worth looking for a job that can teach you business skills as well as pay you a few dollars an hour.

Management Versus Everything Else

The type of job you accept now should, when possible, have some relation to the career you hope to follow in the future.

Many M.B.A. graduates suggest that it's better to work at jobs that teach management skills than it is to work in a setting where you are always being managed by others. While it is difficult to find these positions while you're still in college, any management experience will be helpful to you once business school begins.

The Job-to-Application Connection

After you've finally built up a list of job experiences, the most important thing to do is to make it pay off on your business-school application. When summarizing your work experience in your applications, always be honest, but make your position and responsibility sound as strong as possible. Always make the most of what you've got by listing those details that make it unusual. If you worked sixty hours each week, mention that. If you worked directly with the vice president, be sure to let the business schools know. Work from your strengths; tell the schools what you accomplished, and what you learned from your experience.

Here are some suggestions for other kinds of organizations that offer interesting and valuable jobs for the pre-business student. They can add both depth and variety to your resume.

- *controller's office:* clerical intern in universities or corporations.
- *advertising company:* assistant to a copywriter or account executive
- *foundations:* researcher, office assistant
- *savings banks:* teller, typist
- *corporate businesses:* office intern, accounting, research
- *brokerage houses:* back-office work, phone calling for new accounts
- *city, state, federal government:* budget office positions, research
- *accounting firms:* clerical duties, even accounting if you're an accounting major at college

■ *educational institution:* student teacher in math, economics, etc.

These suggestions are a jumping off point. Any business,
profit-making or nonprofit, can teach you much about working in
the real business world. There's no substitute for observing and
participating in the day-to-day work of a business, and no better
training ground for future executives.

The GMAT and
How to Study for It

How important is the Graduate Management Admission Test? Well, different schools weight it differently when considering applicants, but it is required by almost every business school in the country. This chapter will tell you how to prepare for it, how it is scored, and how it will test your knowledge and skills.

What Is the GMAT?

The GMAT is an exam with eight sections and lasts approximately four hours. Every question is multiple choice. The test is administered in the United States and other countries four times a year (usually in January, March, July, and October).

Other students may have told you that the GMAT predicts your performance in business school. Don't believe it. Similar to the SAT that you took in high school in that it can be studied for, it is by no means an exam which measures natural intelligence.

The exam is divided into two major sections: verbal skills and quantitative skills, and is scored up to a total score of 800. According to the Graduate Management Admission Council and Educational Testing Service, the people who administer this test, two of the eight sections are actually experimental sections whose results don't count toward your score. Unfortunately, the student does not know which two fall into this category until after the test ends. Therefore, you must take each section seriously.

The Types of Questions and How to Answer Them

Within the eight sections of the GMAT, there are five types of questions. The Graduate Management Admission Council describes them as Mathematical Problem Solving, Data Sufficiency, Reading Comprehension, Analysis of Situations, and Verbal Ability. Let's see what these labels mean.

Mathematical Problem Solving

This section measures your math problem-solving ability. You should thoroughly review your high-school geometry and algebra. Your college courses in calculus and statistics will be of no help here, since that material is not on the exam. Calculators and slide rules are not allowed, so you have to rely on your own abilities and a piece of scratch paper. This section includes approximately thirty questions and allows forty minutes for completion.

Data Sufficiency

Many students find this section difficult because it utilizes very unusual rules. Instead of answering the questions and problems that are proposed, you are asked to classify the question under five different categories. The categories are always the same in each problem, so it is important to memorize their order. Every problem states a question that is being asked and then offers two statements that can or cannot answer the question.

After reading the question and the statements, your job is to decide which of the statements is relevant to answering the question. This may sound confusing but it will make more sense when you look at a few sample problems. The five category classifications are: (A)statement one will answer the question, (B)statement two will answer the question, (C)statements one and two will answer the question if used together, (D)either statement used alone will answer the question, and (E)additional information is needed. The directions will always tell you to answer either A, B, C, D, or E. The best preparation for this section is to practice using sample examples in a review book, until you're comfortable with the kind of evaluation for which you're being asked.

Reading Comprehension

This is a part of the verbal section of the GMAT. Similar to the reading comprehension questions on the SAT, this section presents lengthy (and often dry) reading passages for you to study quickly and then answer several questions about. Not only does this section test your comprehension from memory, but it also requires you to draw certain conclusions from the material that you have read.

Be warned that reading these passages is not like skimming a novel or textbooks. These paragraphs have been excerpted from science journals, technical magazines, and so on. In other words, they are written so that you have to *force* yourself to concentrate. No matter how intelligent you are, the *only* way to answer the questions that follow is to read the paragraph carefully and underline pertinent facts—never rely on previous knowledge. The questions are designed to see if you can read difficult material and interpret what you've read. You may be asked about the passage's main idea and even how the information in the passage can be applied to another subject. This section of the exam lasts about thirty minutes.

One way to prepare yourself for these problems is to practice reading similar material and seeing how much you can recall after you have scanned it only once.

Analysis of Situations

Many students find this forty-minute section the most compli-
cated section of the GMAT. The Graduate Management Admission Council states that this section is designed to test your
ability to analyze a management problem once you've been
given certain facts.

Here again, the student reads a long paragraph, which is
sometimes accompanied by a chart. After reading the passage,
you will be given questions to categorize under five different
labels. You must decide which questions are significant to the
manager seeking to solve the problem. In order to do well in
this section of the exam, it is again helpful to memorize the five
categories, so they become second nature and you can answer
each question more quickly. The five categories are: (A)Major
Objective, (B)Major Factor, (C)Minor Factor, (D)Major Assump-
tion, and (E)Unimportant Issue. When you study for this
section, your time will be best spent practicing on the sample
material in the practice booklet and learning the important
but subtle distinctions between the above categories (e.g.,
between a major factor and a major objective).

Verbal Ability

This section tests your writing ability by asking you to read
sentences and decide which part of the sentence is incorrect.
You must read the sentence, which will have four words or
phrases underlined, and decide which one must be changed in
order that the sentence be correctly written in standard English.
However, the sentence may be correct as written, so be careful!
The best way to study for this section is to work with a textbook on grammar and usage, and become secure in your knowledge of good practices. Students we spoke with suggested
trying to read the sentences in this section without paying close
attention to the underlined sections, trying to spot the errors
yourself.

Please note that the GMAT is revised frequently, and you
should check with the *Guide to Graduate Management Educa*

tion for changes in the test's requirements. There are also review books, revised each year, that will provide you with sufficient practice examples.

Registering for the Exam

In order to register for the GMAT, get the brochure from your dean or campus career counseling office. It gives you application dates and other relevant information. This brochure will also explain how the scores are reported to you as well as to the business schools that you designate. With a registration fee and application, you open a file at the testing offices that will hold your GMAT score and other general information useful to the business schools. (If you are out of school or cannot obtain this brochure at your school, write to: Graduate Management Admission Test, Educational Testing Service, Box 966, Princeton, NJ 08541 for information.)

Review Courses and Review Books

Utilize both if you can afford them. Many people take a seven-week or three-week crash course with one of the tutoring services. They can be fairly expensive, but they do provide you with knowledgeable teachers, practice booklets, and tape recordings that will explain the answers. In addition to meeting in a classroom on a daily or weekly basis, you can practice with the booklets during your spare time. As for review books, they are a must for everyone.

Familiarize yourself with the kinds of exam questions. If possible, memorize the directions so that you can use those extra few minutes answering questions.

Test-Taking Strategies

One of the best strategies for doing well on the exam is by practicing with a copy of an actual GMAT. Ask the pre-business adviser if he or she has one on file. Take the test under simulated test-day conditions.

Strategies that you should follow on the day of the exam include the following:

- Try to sleep seven to eight hours during the night before the exam. If you sleep any longer, you'll be lethargic.
- If your exam begins in the morning (it usually does) be awake at least two hours earlier.
- Bring a snack that you can eat during your exam break. High energy foods like nuts or fruit are a good choice.
- Don't sit near nervous and fidgety people during the test. And don't talk to them during the break.
- Don't be afraid to complain if the room is too hot or too cold. If you are uncomfortable it will affect your performance.
- Always ask questions if there is a problem with your test booklet or answer sheet.
- Try to sit next to a wall so that you can turn away from any distractions.
- Bring every possible comfort that will save you time (extra pencils, pencil sharpener, tissues, etc).
- Don't try to show off by finishing first—use all the time you have to check your work.

Canceling the Exam

If, for some reason, you feel that you performed very poorly on the exam, you can cancel it. But you must do this immediately—you don't have the option of seeing your score and then canceling it. While the business schools will know that you canceled the test, it's better to take it again when you're more confident.

Making Your Applications and Essays Stand Out

Many candidates for admission will have good test scores and high grades, so the application and essays give you the valuable opportunity to show how you are unique. Take note that the word here is *unique*—not odd, not outrageous. This strategy will show you how to do more than fill in the blanks and write a few ordinary paragraphs about why you want to attend business school. You will learn how to make the most of what you've got, and show that your application is worthy of notice in the admissions office.

Each business-school application is somewhat different. Some ask very direct questions; other schools prefer to pose open-ended questions that force you to decide what areas to discuss. Whatever the case, the following information should show you how to use each format to your best advantage.

Sending for Applications

While you are in your junior year in college, write to each business school that interests you and ask for a copy of the catalog and the application. It's best to learn as early as possible about the admissions process, the types of questions the schools like to ask, and other information about the business curriculum. Too many students wait until senior year to start reading about the various programs available to them.

The summer before your senior year is the best time to send away for your final applications. (Although applications don't change very much from one year to the next, the ones you received as a junior cannot be used for the following year.) Instead of typing out a formal letter to the admissions office you should simply send a postcard stating your request and providing a return address. The materials are all free so you need not send any money.

It's a good idea to write to at least twelve business schools—it's dangerous to limit yourself to just five or six schools—even if you are at the top of your class.

Once you've requested the applications and financial aid information you'll need (there's a complete list of addresses in the appendix of this book) during the summer before your senior year, you should start receiving some applications by late August or early September.

Two Charts That Will Get You Organized

Before picking up a pen or pencil, read through all of the applications you've received and make sure that all of the pages and forms are there. The last thing you want to do is discover two weeks before the deadline that the application is missing a page. Also, be sure to read through all of the questions before you start writing.

Now draw up a chart like the following one. This "Application-Requirement Chart" will help you place all the information about your applications on one sheet of paper. You will quickly see that there are many details to take care of when dealing with business-school applications. It's not enough to answer some questions and write a few essays—you have to keep up with deadlines for recommendations, transcripts, test scores, as well as various fees that have to be paid. This organizational chart can be used for the entire process, to remind you when to take care of what. If there are any additional concerns that your

Application-Requirement Chart

School	Application Fee	Due Date	Recommendations	Essays	Transcripts	GMAT Scores
Southern Business	$30	Jan. 15	1 employer 2 teachers	5	due Jan. 20	won't accept winter exam
Madison Business	$40	Feb. 1	2 employers 2 teachers	3 required 1 optional	due Feb. 1	accepts winter exam
Carlisle Business	$35	Jan. 15	1 employer 1 teacher	2	due Feb. 1	accepts winter exam
Vernon Business	$35	Feb. 10	employer or teacher or peer	3	due Feb. 10	accepts winter exam

What's-My-Progress Chart

School	Application	Essays	Recommendations	Contacts
Southern Business	finished	all 5 first drafts completed, check grammar	received Prof. Hall's need Prof. Smith's and Ms. Anderson's	Aunt Margaret is an alumnus
Madison Business	need Mom and Dad's social security no.	finish typing required ones. write optional	ask Dean Harrison to photocopy Prof. Hall's	Stacey's Dad used to teach here.
Carlisle Business	ready to be typed	both written and copyread	file is complete	?? ask around
Vernon Business	ask dean about question no. 7d	all 3 are typed. attach an extra essay on summer job	remind Mrs. Black at City Hall	Cousin Jeff used to work for alumni president in 1981

applications pose, allow space for them in your chart. Don't clutter your memory with details when you can write them down and have them at your fingertips.

Now that you've done that, you should photocopy each page of every application form. While it will cost you a few dollars, it's well worth it. Many students make the mistake of putting pen to paper the very minute that they receive an application. Since business schools are looking for flawless applications (without typing mistakes or grammatical errors), it's best to do a first draft on the photocopies.

It might be a good idea to draw up another chart now, which you can later use to record your own progress in the application procedure. While the Application-Requirement Chart tells you what each of the business schools wants from you, the "What's-My-Progress Chart" lets you keep track of if, when, and how you've satisfied those requirements. It's a place where you can jot down the specifics of what you want to include in the essay, whom you've asked to write your recommendations, what's been completed, what needs more work, and so on.

The Application Questions

The first half of most business-school applications is fairly simple. Questions deal with topics ranging from your social security number to your grade point average and your GMAT score. You should be working on a photocopy now, so don't worry about any mistakes.

While you will probably have no difficulty with any of this section, there are certain questions to which you should pay particular attention. You will probably be asked to list your estimated rank in your college class. If you have a good rank, then list it. But if you have a very low rank and are concerned that it might turn off the admissions officers before they get to see the rest of your recommendation, then you may want to leave it blank, or state that you're not certain. Some business schools demand that you list all your numbers (grades, scores) right on the first page of the application. This can be frustrating if you have not tested well but believe your activities, recommendations, and work experience make your application strong. In most cases, the admissions officers will read on, unless they simply have never accepted scores at that level.

Another question you will be asked is whether or not you have received any academic honors. This means you should list special scholastic prizes, such as dean's list, Phi Beta Kappa, and degree with honors. If you've won any of these, list them. If your school doesn't have a dean's list or give other prizes, let the business school know that. Instead of leaving that space blank, use it to say something. Blank spaces frequently speak louder than your answers, so cover yourself.

You will also be asked about your extracurricular activities. Some schools will tell you to list just three or four, and they will leave only about two or three lines of space for you to discuss them. If this is your strong suit, then play it up for all it's worth. Attach an additional page and explain in detail why your activities are important, how many hours you spend on them, and what you've achieved through them.

Business schools are generally most concerned with your work experience. Whether you've been out of school for a few years and maintained a full-time job or whether you are a full-time student with summer and part-time jobs, you should describe your employment background with care. Work experience is important to business schools for various reasons. Your course work in graduate school will be more valuable because your past work experience will give you a frame of reference to help understand the concepts you'll be taught. Business schools want their students to have a realistic grasp of how the business world works, and a clear idea of why they have chosen graduate training in business management.

Questions Not to Answer

You may be faced with a question that you simply don't want to answer, whether you have an answer for it or not. A business school might pose a question that you feel is unfair. An example of this might be a question which asks you to list all the other business schools that interest you. There is absolutely no reason why you should answer this question, because it will tell the school where you rank their program. If a school is your last choice, you don't want them to know that.

Another question that you should consider overlooking is one that asks if you have any problem that may impair your ability to perform well in business school. Any answer but "no" may cause the school to look at you as a liability. A "yes" will force you to offer explanations and excuses that will rarely be acceptable. If you want to go to business school, it should be your own decision. If a physical handicap is involved, you can notify them after admission about special needs like a dormitory room on the ground floor.

Advantage Questions

You may see questions on your application that can work to your advantage. One of these might be a request to list any friends or relatives that attended the business school. Do your best with this. Whether it's a parent, next-door neighbor, or business contact, the alumni connection can usually help. If you're applying to Cornell Business School and your economics professor is a member of the Cornell family, let the admissions people know. If you work at it, you may find a connection to every school.

Another question that may be asked is if you belong to a minority group or have any special background that might distinguish you from the other applicants. Let the school know if you are a member of an ethnic group that has poor representation in the business schools. No matter what kind of academic record you have, you will be given additional consideration by the admissions office.

Shortcuts

Since filling out applications can be tedious and time consuming, it's a good idea to use shortcuts whenever you can. One of the best ways to save time is by going through all of your applications, circling the questions that you can't answer, and then listing them separately. Because some of these questions might require you to contact your parents, the dean, or the registrar, do it all at once.

Another way to save time on the applications is on your essays. You will find that many schools will ask you to write an essay on the same topic.

The Essays

You may be surprised to learn that some business schools ask you to write as many as eight or nine essays for their applications. You will be given directions to keep them a certain length. These essays are all very important, and they should not be written in a hurry. Not only do the essays provide a chance for you to give more details about your experiences and achievements, but they also allow the admissions people to get to know you as an individual.

While some essay questions will be general and ask you just to write about yourself, most will ask specific questions like: Why do you want to attend business school? What are some of your most significant experiences? If you were left on a desert island for two weeks, which three books would you take with you? These are all personal questions that take time to answer. Make sure that not only are you sincere in your answers, but that you provide information that further enhances your application. Many students work for hours to develop an essay that mentions as many of their experiences and activities as possible while also showing how their best personal qualities have developed as a result of those experiences.

Sample Essays

Now you'll read two essays one business school candidate might have written. Although both essays basically provide the same information, they are written in very different styles. The first essay does a poor job of conveying Phil's interest in and aptitude for business. Admissions officers are generally cool on a student who is either ignorant of or nervous about the workings of big business. Maybe you don't have ambitious plans to run a major corporation one day, but it will not help your case to sound modest and unassertive. In this essay Phil appears to lack both confidence and drive when he talks about himself and his accomplishments. When you read the following excerpt from his essay, pretend that you are an employer or an admissions officer (it's been suggested they think the same way). Would you hire him? Do you think he would be a successful candidate for a degree in business management?

A few months ago I decided to apply to business graduate school because it seemed to offer good preparation for an eventual career in business management. Until that point, I followed a standard liberal arts curriculum with a major in Information Sciences.

I think that I could be a good midlevel manager in a major corporation. I haven't had much experience working with other people, but my above-average scores on the GMAT and my good grades in my three economics courses seem to me to indicate that my best career hopes lie in this direction.

My parents helped me get my regular summer job at a small computer sales company in our town (they knew the president from our country club). After a few weeks there I began to get an idea of what the business world was really like, at least on a small scale. I worked a forty-hour week with some overtime, and my main responsibilities were clerical in nature.

I doubt I'll ever reach the level of some of the best-known corporate executives you read about in *Forbes* and *Business Week* (I wouldn't want to cope with *that* kind of stress) but I believe I can make a success of a business career by finding a company I feel I can be happy with, and staying there for the duration of my business career . . .

There is probably not a business school in this country that would find this essay compelling. Even if he was displaying his true nature, what's important to the business schools is not just an applicant's frankness about himself, but his enthusiasm, achievements, and potential to succeed in a high-level business career. This essay would probably have earned Phil a rejection.

The type of essay that will earn a letter of admission from most business schools is one that shows a student's assertiveness and potential for accomplishment in a business career. Most applicants have never held an important position in a corporate hierarchy, but they should try to portray themselves as individuals who have the ambition and desire to be there someday.

No matter how low-key a person you are, there is a way to phrase your essay so that you appear to be ready to tame the world. Business graduate schools appear to welcome the positively aggressive applicant. This is one reason why they are often more eager to accept an applicant who has experienced some of the realities of the business world.

Look at this other version of Phil's essay, and notice how it utilizes the same information as the first essay, but presents the facts in a more positive manner.

After being fascinated by several college courses in economics, I began considering a possible career in business. Because of my superior skills in math, I feel I am well suited for a promising future in finance. The score from my GMAT gave me even more courage to pursue my newfound goal.

Although it may sound rather ambitious, I hope one day to be running a major company in the computer field, and then later founding my own once I've learned the intricacies of managing a staff, raising capital, and predicting the needs of consumers who might be interested in my product. My original interest in the computer industry grew from my work with United Computer Groups Inc. three summers ago. Because it was a rather small company, I had the opportunity to observe all phases of a growing company.

I was so intrigued with my position at United Computers that I found myself working six days a week and ten hours each day sometimes. As a student intern, I learned many office skills and what the day-to-day life of a new business is like.

Reading magazines like *Fortune* and *Forbes* has motivated me to consider my business education as an important investment in my future. I've read about a number of successful executives who have gotten where they are without an M.B.A., but I am convinced that I will be able to go even further after I've finished my graduate business training . . .

Using Recommendations and Contacts to Your Advantage

No matter how outstanding your grades and scores are, you should work to make good use of recommendation letters and contacts when you begin applying to business school. Most schools ask for letters of reference, but you should send them even if they aren't required. Recommendations will provide information about you that the admissions officers generally can't get from your essay or GMAT score.

Whether you plan on applying to a large, prestigious business school or a local, part-time program, begin collecting recommendation letters as early as possible. Since interviews are rarely granted at most business schools, the best facets of your personality, as observed by others, have to come through in a few well-written letters. This strategy will show you how to get the best possible recommendations.

The Purpose of a Recommendation Letter

It takes more than intelligence to get into a good M.B.A. program. You have to display a positive attitude and honest character to the admissions office. But how do you do this if you never meet the admissions committee? By being portrayed in a positive light in a favorable letter of recommendation.

By reading a recommendation letter, admissions officers can see you through your professors' eyes. They know that your teachers, deans, and employers have observed your work, your attitude, and your motivation, and are suited to comment on them. Because business schools encourage students to work as a team, they also want to accept students who work well with others, and your team spirit is something they can't discern by studying your transcript. Since your letters of recommendation will be considered very carefully by the business schools, it's important to try to get the most appropriate people to write them.

Whom to Ask for Recommendations

While it is ideal to begin collecting your letters as early as freshman year, don't worry that you won't get in if it's the beginning of senior year before you start asking people to write on your behalf. You can still ask last semester's history professor or last year's biology instructor for a letter. But do not try to reach back more than two years for someone, especially if you haven't been in contact with them since then. Students who believe that their freshman psychology lecturer will remember them three years later are asking for trouble. If the professor agrees to write, the letter will probably provide few insights to the admissions office.

If you are a recent college graduate or a college senior, your references should always include a few professors from your most challenging courses. If you have been working for several years, you may not be able to get letters from your former professors, so you'll have to rely on some strong letters from employers. Many business schools insist that all applicants have an employer write for them, whether from a summer job experience or a full-time career position. Here are a few more people who may write letters for you:

- pre-business adviser
- co-workers or bosses from jobs you've held
- deans and college administrators
- business people whom you know personally
- alumni from the business school to which you are applying
- a minister or rabbi
- an adviser from one of your activities
- a roommate or close friend

When you ask any of these people to write for you, make certain that the person likes you and knows you well enough to write a personal letter that not only supplies facts, but also conveys the positive aspects of your personality. Don't choose someone just because he or she has a prestigious title. If the person doesn't care enough about you, you may get an unhelpful letter.

How to Ask and How Many to Ask For

Waiting until the last minute to ask for recommendations is one of the worst mistakes you can make. If you give a reference short notice, you may get only a paragraph or two of general remarks, which might turn the admissions people against your otherwise excellent application.

It is wise to collect one or two recommendations at the end of each semester, as soon as grades have been reported. When Tom decided he wanted to go to business school, he was in his sophomore year at college. He waited until he received his grades each semester and then approached the professors he liked best and who gave him good grades. He asked them to forward their individual letters to the pre-business adviser where they could be put on file. By the beginning of his senior year, he had seven letters from different teachers and two letters from his summer job employers to choose from.

Although many schools provide special forms for your letters, some will simply ask you to have someone write, on a separate sheet, about your personality, integrity, and potential as a student. Ask your references to type a two- or three-paragraph letter and then send it to the pre-business adviser, not give it directly to you. Business schools often prefer that applicants be unaware of the comments made in their letters of recommendation.

Making It Easy for the Letter Writer

In order to get the very best recommendation, make it easy for your writer. Don't assume anything. Don't assume that he remembers all your activities, or that he's written dozens of letters in the past. Don't assume that he will remember when and where to mail your letter.

The way to make it easy for your references is to give them a copy of your resume or some other listing of your achievements, activities, and hobbies. Also on this sheet list any specific career interests so that they can be mentioned in the letter. On the top of the page, list the date that the recommendation should be mailed. If you list the day that it's due in the admissions office, your reference will inevitably wait until that day to mail it. Don't take chances.

Sitting down with the reference for a few minutes, politely suggest that you would like the letter to be approximately two to three paragraphs in length, and that it should be typed. Providing an addressed and stamped envelope is a necessary courtesy. A week before it should have been mailed, call and say thank you. This will not only show your appreciation, but also will remind your reference to complete the task if it hasn't been done already.

How to Screen the Recommendations

Since most business schools ask that your letters be sent directly from the writer to the dean or pre-business adviser, you will never see them. Although some professors will give you a copy of their letters, most will not. One way to make sure that a bad or mediocre recommendation is not forwarded by the pre-business adviser or dean is to ask them to select the two or three best letters from your file. This is why it is important to have at least four or five different letters to choose from.

Alumni Contacts

Although they should never be used in lieu of teacher or employer recommendations, alumni recommendations can add to your application if they are well written and especially if the writer is an alumnus who is still actively involved with the particular school. Remember that an alumnus only has power at one school, his or her own. Because of this, you should have alumni write directly to the school and bypass the pre-business adviser.

If your alumni reference wants to call the admissions office, that's fine, but encourage him or her to write as well. A letter is a permanent record of support.

How to Get a Poor
Letter of Recommendation

There are always students who end up being rejected by business schools because they don't take the proper precautions when asking for letters of recommendation. Here are four ways to elicit a negative letter:

- Ask a person who has no respect for you or your achievements.
- Persuade an unwilling person to write for you.
- Insist that the reference mention certain things in his or her letter.
- Ask someone who does not like you personally.

There are actually students who've committed all of these mistakes. They ended up with tersely worded notes and obviously negative letters.

How to Get a Mediocre Letter of Recommendation

Another type of recommendation stands halfway between a negative letter and a positive endorsement of an applicant. Mediocre letters are a common occurrence in admissions offices. These letters, while they rarely speak against a student, almost never help his case. You will get a mediocre letter if you:

- Ask a professor who gave you an average grade (B or less).
- Approach an employer whom you haven't seen in three or more years.
- Choose a reference who is not very articulate.
- Ask a professor who knows nothing or little about your life outside of the classroom.

The problem with mediocre letters is that they tell the admissions officer that you were not an outstanding student or employee. Perhaps you did moderately well in this class or on that job, but you didn't distinguish yourself in any way. Graduate schools are not looking for "moderately good" students.

How to Get a Positive Letter of Recommendation

If you've followed the advice in this chapter, you should have no problem eliciting a positive letter from each of your references. While it may take a little more time to find the best people to ask, it will make a difference in the end. Here is what you should do in order to attract winning letters:

- Only request a recommendation from someone who is enthusiastic about writing for you.
- Ask a teacher who knows about your classroom performance *and* your extracurricular activities.
- Choose a writer who thinks you are superior to most other employees or students.
- Ask a person who honestly believes you would make a good business executive.

As long as you don't procrastinate in your hunt for good letters, you should have no problem using letters of recommendation to strengthen your application.

Dealing with Parents

Chances are your parents never dreamed of raising a child who would become an M.B.A. candidate. If they were ambitious for you, more likely they were expecting you to attend law or medical school. But no matter what your parents' expectations were, and no matter how much you're not inclined to fulfill them, it's helpful to understand how they are feeling during this time.

Just as you worry about rejection, they too worry about it. What makes it especially difficult for your parents is that they probably don't understand how the selection and application process works. In order to keep them from calling you each day to ask, "Have you heard yet?", sit down and explain that there are many components involved: your grades, GMAT score, application, essays, and letters of recommendation. Some parents may assume that there is some single all-important factor to getting accepted to or rejected from graduate school.

Tell them that many schools don't respond until late April. While you will probably hear sooner, telling them this will ease the tension when it gets to be that time. If they think you're telling them everything, they will relax a little.

Unfortunately, though, there are other parents who are not willing to relax so quickly. These parents need special handling.

The Let-Me-Check-Over-All-Your-Applications-Before-Mailing Parent

Although this parent gives you the impression that she doesn't think you're capable of completing a perfect application by yourself, don't let it offend you. Say that you appreciate the concern, but that it is against the rules for anyone except the student to work on the application. If she insists, send her a photocopy and say that you will consider all corrections. Having a parent like this isn't all bad—at least she can catch your spelling mistakes.

The Don't-Apply-Because-We-Can't-Afford-Business-School Parent

It's hard to be upset with this parent because he is trying to act in what (he thinks) is your best interest. He doesn't want you to apply and then get your hopes up if he can't afford to send you to the school. Be understanding with the parent who tells you not to apply because of financial reasons, and explain that all of the business schools to which you're applying offer financial aid to those who need it. Tell him that you will not attend a school that will not help you find the grants and loans you will need.

The You-Must-Go-to-Business-School-Whether-You-Like-It-or-Not Parent

This can be the most frustrating situation, and you have to try to handle it firmly. If you have no desire to get an M.B.A. you're wasting your time going through the application process. There are some parents who may try to force a particular career on their children, and this can be quite damaging. Try to reason with your parents and explain that they will be wasting their money on something you don't want. Many parents will see your side when they realize that business school can cost as much as $12,000 per year.

If money isn't an issue, and your parents won't listen to your arguments, you may decide to go through the motions. Unless you give it your best shot, your low GMAT score and lackluster applications will probably assure that you get rejected. If this is the only way to handle the problem, then it's up to you.

The You-Haven't-Got-a-Snowball's-Chance Parent

Then there are the parents who are totally unsupportive. Ignore them. They may be displaying this attitude in order to prepare themselves for a rejection, or (more likely) because they are slyly trying to motivate you. If a parent tells a child that he'll never be able to do something, the child usually tries twice as hard to accomplish what he's been challenged to do. Tell your parents that you disagree with them, and that you'll do your best to prove them wrong.

The Alma Mater Parent

If you happen to be the son or daughter of a mother or father who has an M.B.A., it's a good idea to consider applying to his or her school. The alumni connection can be very important because schools often accept members of the same family. This is part of the reason they attract donations from their graduates. While it's not guaranteed that you'll be accepted, the odds are in your favor.

How Parents Can Help

While it's wrong to let your parents write your essays or fill out your applications, there are many ways that they can work with you on the business school application process. You can use your parents as sounding boards as you write your essays. Ask them if you sound too pompous or too modest. Get them to read over each application and to look for mistakes or omissions. They may enjoy being a part of the process.

Ten Mistakes to Avoid While Applying

There is a wide margin for error when coping with the business school application process. Since there are so many components to take care of and points to keep in mind, mistakes can occur very easily. This strategy will warn you against the ten most common mistakes that the business-school applicant may make. If you forget everything else that you've learned in this book, at least remember to avoid doing the following:

1. *Nagging the admissions office to grant you a personal interview.*

You will not only be wasting your time trying to convince the admissions people to interview you, but you will be wasting *their* time. And you can rest assured that they will remember anyone who tries to infringe on their time or bucks their system. There are informational interviews available at some schools, but it is next to impossible to receive an evaluative interview unless you know someone personally in the admissions office. If you make yourself a pest, it could influence the readers of your application when it comes up for discussion.

2. *Taking the GMAT without preparing for it.*

Although not everyone takes a review course or buys a study manual, no one should walk into these marathon exams without first becoming familiar with the format and the directions. Not only does this test force you to work under pressure, but it requires you to recall certain mathematical concepts that you may have learned several years before. This exam does not measure natural intelligence, so don't walk into the examination room without preparing yourself.

3. *Lying or stretching the truth in an application.*

People who lie on their applications usually don't get away with it. No matter how much it appears to improve your record, misrepresenting activities or other achievements can ruin your chances for admission if anyone suspects you. It's a small world and you'd be surprised how many admissions officers know your deans and fellow classmates. There are just too many ways for people to check on what you write, so be honest.

4. *Being too modest about your achievements.*

Business school doesn't admire modesty in its applicants. Don't be afraid to sell yourself. If you've got a strong background, it won't help you to hide it or to avoid drawing attention to it. If you believe that the admissions people will somehow recognize your ability and admit you, you're wrong. Either they will overlook your achievements or they will criticize you for not recognizing the value of your own talents. The only way to gain respect for your achievements is to highlight them. Not only does this highlighting show that you are proud of your accomplishments, but it will distinguish you from other applicants.

5. *Applying to too few schools.*

If you're overly confident or too thrifty, you will inevitably make this mistake. Every year, there are students who declare that they are certain to get into all of the top five business schools—so naturally they only bother applying to those five. Then they happen to get rejected from all five. You should definitely apply to at least three or four schools beside your "top five." Since you'll have to wait an entire year to apply again, if you've been rejected, it's smarter to apply to nine or ten schools the first time around.

6. *Letting fellow classmates look at your completed application.*

By the time you get halfway through the application process, you will understand the true meaning of the word *anxiety*. Much of the tension exists because your classmates are all competing against one another. Many people, including your roommates and close friends, may ask to look at your applications.

Whether it's because they want to give advice, check for errors, or simply to see how you've portrayed yourself, don't show the application to them. After spending several hours on an original essay, you don't want to take the risk that a classmate will borrow the idea for his or her own application.

7. *Calling the admissions office before the notification date to ask if you've gotten in yet.*

There are many reasons why it may take a long time for you to hear from the different schools. Scores could have been sent late from the GMAT office. One of your recommendations might have arrived late. You can create a bad name for yourself by nagging the admissions office for notification. Even if friends and relatives continue to ask you each day about the status of your application, you must resist the temptation of calling the schools.

If other students hear from one of your schools two weeks before you do, don't become paranoid. If you're a definite "reject," you'll probably hear before anyone else, so just be patient.

8. *Waiting until the last minute to collect letters of recommendation.*

Proscrastinating comes easily to all of us. Unfortunately, so will disappointing recommendations if you're not careful. Since your recommendations are supposed to convince the admissions people that you're worthy of a closer look, you must do everything you can to elicit positive, well-written letters. The secret to doing this is making good use of time in every possible way. Always give people at least two or three weeks to write a letter, more if possible. If they feel rushed, it will be detected in the tone of their writing.

Once you've decided who will write your recommendations, make sure that the envelope you supply is addressed properly. And be sure to ask your reference to type the letter.

9. *Being too creative in your application and essay.*

Although many business schools claim that they are trying to diversify their student body by admitting more and more liberal arts students, don't assume that they will respond to outrageous application gimmicks. They don't want any gourmet angel food cakes or hybrid rose bushes. You want to stand out, but being too creative in a nonprofessional manner can work against your chances for admission.

It's important to stress your talents, personal qualities, and special interests, but you don't want to come off as an oddball.

10. *Forgetting to photocopy the completed application and not having it sent by certified mail.*

No matter how careful you are while filling in the application, your work will all go down the drain if you forget to photocopy the essays and questions once you're done. Mailing each application by certified mail (with a return receipt requested) guarantees that it has arrived safely. If there are ever any problems, and the admissions office needs another copy of what you sent them, your photocopy will come in handy.

From the Inside:
The Admissions Officer's
Perspective

There are probably some questions that you might like to ask admissions officers if you had the chance. In most cases you will never get to meet these people. There are rarely admissions interviews, and they do not invite applicants to phone at their leisure when a special problem or question arises. We've tried to supply the answers to some common questions about the admissions process by speaking with admissions officers from Pace Business School, Harvard Business School, and the Business School at the State University of New York at Albany.

Does the business school admissions committee include faculty and students, or is it limited to staff admissions officers?

Albany: We do not use students to aid in the decisions. Selection is usually made by the admissions staff, unless we come across a difficult, borderline case. In those situations, we use an additional faculty committee. We may even ask the applicant to come in for an interview when we feel it is necessary.

Harvard: Students are not involved. The selections are made by the admissions staff only.

Pace: Students and faculty members do not become involved in our selection process, which is handled solely by admissions staff.

*Many students believe that business schools have strict require-
ments for their applicants. Do you use grade point average and
GMAT cut-offs when you consider a student's transcript?*

Harvard: We use no cut-off numbers.

Albany: While we use no formal cut-off points, we do use the
combined scoring system that is provided by the Graduate Management Admission Council. We never go below 950 and rarely
accept students with a score of below 1100. But we must take
into account more than just the numbers. We consider the
application, essays, and references of each applicant.

Pace: We do not use any cut-off points for grades and scores.

*There is some confusion about taking the GMAT more than
once. When a student takes it the first time and receives a low
score, then takes it a second time and receives a higher score,
which score do you use when deciding whether or not to admit
the student?*

Pace: We average the scores and use that number.

Harvard: We average the scores.

Albany: We always take the highest score.

*Many applicants assume that the professors and other people
who recommend them will only write positive letters of recommendation for them. Do you ever receive "recommendations"
that are blatantly negative?*

Albany: Some letters we receive will not say anything positive
at all. Others are merely two or three lines. With most letters,
we examine what's actually been said, not just whether it's
positive or negative. Although it doesn't happen very often, we
occasionally receive obviously negative letters.

Harvard: We rarely receive blatantly negative letters.

Pace: Yes, we have received negative "recommendations" for
some applicants from time to time.

Would you ever turn down a student who has a top grade point average and a perfect GMAT score?

Harvard: We've turned down applicants with these credentials many times. We often get students who apply with perfect grades and scores, and don't accept all of them.

Albany: I have never seen perfect scores, but I have seen scores of 750. What is important to us is that we accept students who are not just top academic performers, but also people who will contribute to the program. A problem arises when we see an applicant who has high scores and low grades. The score shows us that the person has the ability, but we wonder if the student worked hard enough in school. This is when I will take it a step further and invite the applicant to the school for an interview.

Many prospective applicants take time off to work before business school. Do you care about the type of employment that they have held?

Pace: We certainly care about their employment records if they've been working for several years. Since these applicants may not score as well on the GMAT as graduating college seniors, we want to take everything into consideration. Their special talents may be discovered in their jobs.

Harvard: We definitely care about an applicant's work experience because we want more than just to select good classroom students. We are looking for people who will make good general managers after graduation.

Albany: Work experience is important if the applicant's other credentials are not so strong. We are looking for the well rounded candidate, whether it's someone who majored in humanities or some other field. Although we look at work experience, we look at many other areas.

Many older people may be discouraged from applying to business school because they think that the M.B.A. program is only for the younger, recently graduated college student. Is this true?

Harvard: It's not true at all. Our age range of incoming students generally spans from twenty to forty years old. Many of them have worked for several years.

Pace: There are certainly no biases against age. We have accepted many students who are fifty years of age and older.

Albany: Just last year, we had a class of students that ranged in age from twenty-two to fifty-three years old.

Some students are concerned about waiving their rights to seeing the recommendations that are written for them when they apply to business school. Do you hold it against a student if he refuses to waive his rights? Does it matter to you?

Pace: It does not matter to us if a student waives his rights or not.

Albany: Actually we would like applicants to waive their rights so that the references feel free to write as they wish.

Harvard: It does not matter if the student waives his rights.

Do you take into account the fact that applicants come from different undergraduate schools when you compare grades on different transcripts? If one applicant graduated from Yale and another applicant graduated from a less competitive college, how do you compare the grading?

Harvard: We are aware of the differences between colleges, but we don't attempt to normalize each candidate's transcript on the basis of the college he attended.

Pace: The quality of college that a student graduates from counts a lot in the selection process.

Albany: I'm not so sure that a B at one college is different from a B at another. We look for students from good schools, but we need a better reason to accept them. We want to know that they worked hard, no matter which college they attended.

After Getting Accepted
or Rejected

Whether you're a pessimist or an optimist, it's a good idea to prepare yourself both for rejection and acceptance. Business school admissions is quite different from undergraduate admissions, so you should know what may happen.

To begin with, there may be several different notification dates at each school, depending on how early you mailed your application. In fact, at some schools, students can be accepted or rejected anytime between the day the application is received by the business school and the day before business school begins its new school year in September.

Acceptances

If your business schools have staggered dates, you can be assured that it is to your advantage to send your application in at the earliest possible date, before the entire class is selected. Your application will probably be considered as soon as it arrives at the office, and you will often receive a response within five or six weeks. Some schools will notify their applicants as soon as late October or early November.

Since most applicants do not hear from their schools until March or April, the admissions office doesn't require an acceptance deposit or a promise to matriculate until the beginning of May.

Waiting List

Then there's the uncertainty of the waiting list. Some business schools will admit a certain number of students and then place a smaller number of applicants on the waiting list as alternates because they are good candidates, but not as strong as those who were accepted. Once some of the accepted students decide not to attend the school, the wait-listed students are given a place in the class.

Unfortunately, you rarely have an idea of where on the list you've been placed. If you are second or third on the list, you probably have nothing to worry about, but if you're number fifty-three, you may not get in at all. Most schools never let you know where you stand, so the only thing you can do is send in more information or additional recommendations that may improve your chances of being put onto the stack of acceptances.

Rejections

Like acceptances, rejection letters can also be mailed to students very early in the selection process. If you are a definite "no" candidate, the admissions people won't hesitate to forward a rejection letter quickly.

Remember that no matter how many business schools reject your application, you should not take the turndowns personally. It can be an emotionally charged time in your life, but try to keep in mind that the business school is turning down your professional qualifications—not you as a person. Each business school may interpret your activities, your courses, your recommendations, your summer jobs, and your essays differently.

If you happen to be rejected, don't think that you can swear your friends to secrecy. Since bad news spreads fast, it's probably best to only tell your family about your disappointment.

The worst thing you can do after being rejected is to get on the telephone and call the business school admissions office

Many students feel that they can pin the admissions officer down and find out exactly why they were not accepted. You will not be successful with this method. If you must know, have the pre-business adviser call for you; or, if you're out of school, write and request an explanation so that you can try to improve your application next time.

Reapplying After Rejection

When you completed your applications, you probably noticed a question that asked if you had ever applied to and been rejected by the school before. Answering "yes" to this question won't help your application, but if you do so, you must follow it up by making a strong case for the school to decide to admit you this time.

There are three reasons why you might reapply to a school after previously being rejected. One reason is that the school itself suggests that you reapply after waiting one or two years. They usually want you to work for that length of time and gain business experience. A second reason is that you feel you have a more impressive record to present (maybe you've taken the GMAT again and raised your score or won a prestigious fellowship). A last reason might be that you feel that the admissions office rejected you in error.

Improving Your Record
After Being Wait-Listed

If there is any time to try and add credentials to your record, it once you've been placed on a school's waiting list. It's a do or die period when you may try to raise your GMAT score, improve your grade point average, become the president of a new activity, submit an unusually strong recommendation, and so on. You may never have another chance, so do whatever you

can to make your case look better than those of the other
candidates.

Deferrals

Some business schools use what they call a deferred acceptance,
where they accept a student but tell him or her not to begin
classes for another two years. Schools use this type of acceptance when they want a student to work in the business world
and gain more "real world" skills before taking part in the
classroom experience graduate school offers. This is still an
acceptance, so make your plans accordingly.

Getting the Decision Reversed

Most admissions officers will tell you that it may not be done,
but it is possible to get a rejection reversed at some schools. If
you can prove that the school was not given correct information
(e.g., your school sent the wrong transcripts or your most
recent GMAT score was never received), then your case might
be reconsidered. Speak to your dean and have him or her
contact someone in the school admissions office. Since mistakes
can happen, decisions can be changed.

Another method for getting a decision reversed (and this
strategy can only be used in a few schools) is doing it politically.
If you have important strings to pull, you should pull them now.
Of course, you should have done this before, but it may not be
too late. There's no guarantee, but important contacts can sometimes help reverse a negative decision.

How to Pay for Business School

Although some companies will reimburse tuition costs for their employees' M.B.A. degrees, many students are not in this position. If you are finishing college and beginning business school, or if you work for a company whose benefits do not include help with your tuition, this strategy is for you.

Business school is not cheap. Whether you attend one of the large, prestigious schools or one that is funded by your state, your expenses can range from $2500 to $9000 for tuition alone each year. If you're living away from home, you have to consider the cost of room and board as well as the cost of books and travel.

If you need financial aid, don't hesitate to apply for it. In many schools, at least 50% of the student body is receiving some form of financial aid. Although some of the forms have different names and many of the procedures change when funds are depleted, business schools offer loans, grants, scholarships, and work-study opportunities for those who qualify.

Loan Programs

Since the provisions for the different loan programs are constantly changing, your first stop should be your university's or a business school's financial aid office.

One of the most popular loan programs is the Guaranteed

Student Loan (GSL). You may have heard of this under the name Federally Insured Student Loan (FISL) or the Higher Education Loan Program (HELP). The loan is called "FISL" if the money is administered by the federal government, and "GSL" if administered by a state agency. The most that you can borrow under this program is $25,000.

You must check into whether you have already borrowed under this program during college. If so, check to be sure you haven't used the entire $25,000. As of the publication of this book, these loans are available to any student whose family income does *not* exceed $30,000. They are also available to students whose family income exceeds $30,000 if they can show financial need (based on size of family, other family members in school, and so on). Under these loans, there are also provisions for students who have an independent status from their parents. In order to declare independent status, a student has to be living on his or her own without receiving financial support for at least a year before application for the loan. There are other requirements that you can find out about by checking with the financial aid office at your school or the business school.

Although these loans don't have to be paid back until you're finished with business school, the interest rates can be set at either 7%, 8%, or 9%, depending on when you began your first FISL or GSL loan. This loan can be repaid over a period of up to nine or ten years. In order to apply for these loans, you should speak to a loan officer at a bank in your area. The business schools have nothing to do with the granting of these loans.

National Direct Student Loans

Another loan program available is the National Direct Student Loan (NDSL), which many students take advantage of while in college. Although the provisions for this loan have changed in the past, the total loan available to each student from the program is $12,000. The interest rate is set at 5% and can be paid back over a period of up to ten years.

Federal "Plus" Loans

This third type of loan can provide business school students with up to $3,000 each year, no matter how wealthy their families happen to be. There is a catch. The "plus" loans are provided at commercial rates of interest. In addition, the lending bank can require you to begin repayment while you're still in school. Your parents are ultimately responsible for these loans.

State Loans

It is also a good idea to research what special loan programs your state has to offer. While most loan money comes from the federal government, some states have loans for students. Ask a local bank officer for advice.

The GAPSFAS Form

This financial statement is provided by the Graduate and Professional School Financial Aid Service (GAPSFAS) or the Educational Testing Service. The GAPSFAS form is a relatively simple, yet visually confusing four-page questionnaire. It provides clear directions on how to answer the various financial questions, although some students are discouraged from applying for financial aid to schools because of the time it may take to fill it out properly.

You will need to complete this form if you want your school to consider awarding you any form of financial aid. For the GAPSFAS form, you will need your parents' income tax form as well as your own.

Borrowing from the Business School

Unfortunately, some students are refused loans from their banks. If this happens to you, your business school can probably act as a lender. It will require you to submit a GAPSFAS form and perhaps other information if you want it to obtain the loans for you. The business school financial aid office can provide you with more information. Instead of repaying the government program directly, you may have to repay the school.

Special Grants and Scholarships

Because corporations are frequently looking for talented young M.B.A. graduates, they take a special interest in the various business schools. Many of them display their interest by setting up special scholarships or fellowships in their names. They will usually allow the private institution to select the student who receives the award.

Many other corporations, foundations, and private endowments work independently of the business school. They might sponsor small or large scholarships that students can compete for through special exams or essay-writing contests. There are even special grants for students who happen to be residents of certain counties or cities.

The best way to learn about these additional resources is to ask each business school to send you its brochures on special scholarships. They aren't likely to send this information to students who are too shy to ask for it.

Work-Study Programs

A very popular method by which students can help pay for business school is a work-study plan administered by your school's financial aid office. Because there are generally many jobs available on campus (in the library, dining hall, departmental offices, for example), the school will help you pay your tuition by providing you with some sort of employment. Because business school requires a great amount of time for class preparation, most work-study programs allow first-year students to work at a paying job for about ten to fifteen hours each week. By the second year, however, some students are able to work as much as twenty to twenty-five hours each week.

In addition to figuring the money earned from the above program into your financial aid package, the business school assumes that you will be earning money during the summer. Each student is expected to contribute a certain amount of money from his or her summer earnings.

Scholarship Search Services

In the past few years, several companies have emerged to help students who are in need of financial aid. The scholarship search companies utilize computers to research special scholarships available to various students. By taking specific information about the student (ethnic background, religion, sex, special interests) and entering it into the computer, the search service can locate scholarship programs that are looking for students with similar backgrounds. The service will then give the student a list of addresses to write to in order to apply for the specific scholarship programs. Many large cities have companies like this that charge a reasonable fee for the service.

When searching for financial aid, don't wait until the last minute. Because funds are limited in most programs, they may run out before you apply.

Surviving Your Years at Business School

Should I have taken math in college? Are the other students very competitive? Are there benefits to going part-time? When do I choose a business-school concentration? How does the case method work? Does class participation count? How do students interview for jobs?

These are just a few of the questions that students may be asking as they prepare to apply to business school. The best way to learn what the business school experience is like is either to live it ourselves or to speak with students who are already there. This chapter features interviews with four students currently attending business school.

In order to provide a wide range of viewpoints, the students—Juli, Nancy, Young Suk, and Judy—represent four different concentrations in the business curriculum. Each student is concentrating in one of the four following areas: marketing, accounting, finance, and computer services. Three of the students are studying full-time at an Ivy League business school and one is studying part-time in a top ten business school while maintaining a full-time job.

Do you need to know a lot of economics and math in order to survive the first year of school?

Juli: I took only one economics course in college, and have taken no math since high school, and I'm doing fine. You just have to be comfortable with numbers.

Nancy: It helps if you have a quantitative mind. But some schools put less of an emphasis on numbers.

How are your final grades computed?

Young Suk: It's very different from law school, where everything depends on your final exam. At business school, there are usually frequent homework assignments which are graded. Students also get graded on class participation.

Nancy: Many schools have midterm exams, so the student has an idea of how well he or she is doing before the final exam takes place.

Are there advantages to attending business school part-time?

Judy: Although I can only take one or two courses at a time, I'm able to earn a good salary from my job during the day. My company will reimburse me for some of the courses. I'm glad I'm working now because I'm learning more from a "real world" job than I ever could by going to school, alone.

Describe how the case method works in business school.

Nancy: Although some business schools teach pure theory, some of them like to train students by giving them actual annual reports and balance sheets from corporations. They ask us to study them, present the cases in an oral format, and then discuss what we might have done to solve a particular company problem.

Which year is harder in business school?

Young Suk: The first year is definitely harder. The second year is easier because by then you've learned what's important and what isn't. You learn how to form study groups. Since there is an overlap between some courses, you learn the material faster.

Nancy: I don't know which year of business school is harder, but I know I work harder here than I did in college.

How do people prepare for exams?

Nancy: I have a study group that meets twice a week. Business school is a group effort and it's a good idea to find two or three other serious students to study with. Sometimes old exams are on file so you can look at those.

Young Suk: Some people try to cram at the end of the semester, but there's just too much to study. Save all your write-ups and notes from each class because they come in handy for the second year of classes.

What do most students dislike about business school?

Juli: It's annoying when some college economics majors and accounting students take the basic courses to get top grades and ruin the grading curve on purpose.

Young Suk: Many students dislike the accounting courses, but they are very important. Also, people are sometimes upset because business school is much more impersonal than college. People here are forced to compete because they feel everyone will be applying for the same jobs in the end.

Nancy: Many people who have worked for a year or more before school dislike having to do homework each night.

Judy: Students who attend part-time complain that it takes too many years to receive their degrees. Sometimes I think it may take me seven or eight years to finish this degree.

How should college students prepare for business school? Should they major in economics?

Nancy: I know I had an advantage since I took finance, marketing, and economics courses in college. Now I'm using some of the same books in business school. Take accounting in college.

Juli: You don't have to major in math or economics. I was an architecture major in college.

Young Suk: College students can major in whatever they want, but they should learn writing skills and take some courses in economics so that they become familiar with business terminology.

Are grades important to employers?

Young Suk: I don't think grades are very important when you are job hunting, especially when you come from a good school. I have had many job interviews, but only one employer has asked for my grades. The employers who are most concerned with grades are the prestige consulting and investment banking groups.

Nancy: Grades are not very important for most jobs. I have a friend at a top ten business school with straight A's and he still couldn't find a summer job.

Juli: What I hear from other students is that grades are only important to employers who are hiring for investment banking and consulting firms. I haven't heard the same about my area of interest. I am concentrating in marketing and planning to go into advertising.

Do you have time for a social life while in business school?
Nancy: You make time. I try to take off one day each weekend.
Juli: I certainly have some free time. Some people even have enough time to hold a part-time job while going to school.

Do you wish you had worked before attending business school?
Young Suk: I'm glad I went directly to business school after college. Fortunately, I knew what I wanted out of business school. If you know what you want, then you should not be intimidated into working first.

Juli: I have no regrets about not working first. Some of the older students look down on us and say we're not serious, but it doesn't bother me.

Nancy: I worked for one year at a brokerage firm on Wall Street before coming to business school and I'm glad I did. It showed me what the real world was like. My job showed me that few people will take a woman seriously when she's working on Wall Street without an M.B.A.

What is the job-hunting process like for business-school students?
Nancy: Each fall, company representatives visit the campus and give presentations to the students. They hold many lavish receptions for us, and they set up individual interviews in the career placement office.

Young Suk: There is a lottery system used in order to distribute the half-hour interviews with employers. If you do well in the first interview, you will get a call-back. Many companies will fly you to their main offices and pay for your transportation and hotel expenses. I think a student's personality is very important when an interviewer is trying to hire a new employee. They want a person who is intelligent and who will fit into the corporate image.

Six Myths (and Six Facts)
About the Career of an M.B.A.

Because the M.B.A. is still a considerably new degree, there are many misconceptions about the type of career it can promise. Many people underestimate its power, while still others overestimate its ability to turn a career around. Just so that you are not caught by surprise after two years of graduate school, it's a good idea for you to read about some of the common myths surrounding the career that an M.B.A. degree will provide.

In order to correct some of these myths, we will be hearing from two former M.B.A. students who are now working after graduating a few years ago. Gary went to business school directly after graduating from college. Sharon went to business school several years after finishing college and working in the business world.

MYTH #1: *Once you receive an M.B.A., you will no longer have to look for employers. They will be looking for you.*

FACT: The M.B.A. graduate is no longer such a rarity that employers are fighting to hire him or her away with outrageous salary offers. While there are certainly jobs out there, the degree alone is not going to get you any one that you want.

Sharon: "Many people don't realize it, but all M.B.A. graduates aren't given the same consideration. After concentrating in marketing, I learned that information services and computers is where most of the jobs are. In addition to that, students should know that some companies don't recruit at certain business schools. The large, prestigious schools will attract a greater number of quality employers."

Gary: "I remember that it was very difficult finding a summer job during business school. I got mine through a friend of my professor. Even if you're in business school, you have to use contacts like you would for any other job. And even when you get interviews, you can have a tough time. Full-time interviewing started in January of the second year and took up a lot of time from your classwork and personal life. It's a big time commitment on the student's part."

MYTH #2: *What you study in business school is almost identical to the work you will be performing as an M.B.A. graduate.*

FACT: This is not necessarily true, because your job may be administrative and you may have attended a school with a heavily theoretical curriculum. There is also the possibility that you will concentrate in one area of business, and then later accept a job in another area.

Gary: "I'm working for a major oil company, and I've used a lot of my school training since I started my job. There is one major difference, though, and that is that I am using a lot more accounting on my job than I was ever taught. Although I could have taken more accounting courses, I didn't. I didn't realize I would need so much."

Sharon: "Although I am now working for a computer services company, I was a marketing major at business school. You may not always be able to find a job that fits in directly with what you were studying in school."

MYTH #3: *If you're already out in the business world, and have decided to get an M.B.A., your salary will no doubt be raised a great deal once you get the degree.*

STRATEGY #16: SIX MYTHS (AND SIX FACTS)
ABOUT THE CAREER OF AN M.B.A.

95

FACT: Many people get an M.B.A. because they want to learn new skills or because they want to change careers. Some employers may not feel that an M.B.A. degree is going to make you worth more money to them. Some may not care whether you have the degree or not.

Sharon: "I honestly believe that I could have gotten my present job even if I didn't have an M.B.A."

MYTH #4: *Business school is very similar to other types of graduate schools in that it teaches you more complex theories than you learned on an undergraduate level.*

FACT: Business school is actually what some like to call "an expensive trade school for ambitious and intelligent people." Because many schools use the case method, it's becoming more and more like the real world and less like the theoretical frameworks of other graduate schools.

Gary: "The thing I disliked about business school was that it was so practical, some people didn't care about learning. Many people were there only to get jobs. Some of them even clustered in cliques according to the types of career plans they had. The investment banking and management consulting people would usually hang out together because they were the prestige-career people."

MYTH #5: *If you don't want to live in New York or Los Angeles, big business is probably not for you.*

FACT: This myth is incredibly common and may therefore turn away many potential M.B.A. applicants. They have this notion that all M.B.A. graduates move to either New York or Los Angeles to find a promising job. Not only are there large corporations that have main offices and branches in small cities, but there are many prospering businesses in suburban and near-rural areas.

Gary: "Although I finally accepted a job in New York, I have worked in the Chicago office. I previously interviewed for good jobs in smaller cities like Washington, D.C."

Sharon: "I wanted to remain in the suburbs and I eventually accepted a position in a relatively small town."

MYTH #6: *Employers who are looking for M.B.A. graduates will generally play fair in an interview. Since they know you are intelligent, they will show respect and try to make you comfortable.*

FACT: Employers are human and they will very often ask whatever they want when interviewing a candidate.

Sharon: "Although they aren't supposed to do it, some employers asked me about my husband and child. I was totally honest, but it did surprise me that they would ask personal questions."

Gary: "I remember interviewing with investment banks and I hated it. They asked personality questions. I much preferred questions that tested your knowledge—like those that presented a practical problem that needed to be solved."

The Get-into-Business-School Calendar

The business school admissions process is much more compli-
cated than you probably expected when you began this book.
You no longer have a guidance counselor who will send in all of
the necessary material to the admissions office. But fortunately
there is a way to make all of the right moves while you're in
college. Beginning as early as freshman year or as late as senior
year (but try not to wait until then), the "Get-into-Business-
School Calendar" will help you handle all the important steps of
building a good record of activities, meeting with advisers,
choosing courses, and taking exams.

If you follow this calendar, you won't have to constantly
search for registration dates or information on when to begin
your applications, collect your recommendations, or search for
financial aid. This schedule will organize everything in the proper
order.

Freshman Year

September–October
Meet with your new academic adviser and pre-business adviser
and make a tentative schedule of college courses for the next
two years. Explore clubs, sports, and other extracurricular
activities. Visit the career placement office and pick up some
business-school catalogs. Save them for future reading.

November–December
Now that you're settled into your classes, develop a good rapport with your professors by contributing to class discussion. Remember, you'll be asking them for recommendations later. Organize a study group or find a tutor to prepare for your first finals.

January–February
Keep up with pre-business information by joining the pre-business society. If you haven't done so already, stop by the dean's or president's office and introduce yourself. Even if you just want to tell them that you like your courses, they will appreciate it and remember your comments.

March–April
Meet with your adviser again and plan your courses for next year. Consider including an economics course if you didn't take one during your first year. Keep your college's distribution requirements in mind. Begin making your summer plans (summer school, job in a bank, travel).

May–June
Approach your favorite professors from this year and ask them for letters of recommendation. Have them send the letters to the pre-business adviser or the dean's files. Prepare for finals and limit your time spent on extracurricular activities.

July–August
Use the summer to read through those business-school catalogs and applications to see what questions they ask. Before finishing your summer job, ask your boss for a written recommendation. Send a thank-you note to the employer—this may help you get a job there again next summer.

Sophomore Year

September–October

Make good first impressions on new professors and start new courses with enthusiasm. Continue last year's activities or join others, but try to concentrate on just a couple. Aim for a leadership position in one of your activities.

November–December

Consider attending one of the M.B.A. Forums that the Graduate Management Admission Council sponsors. Read more business-school catalogs. Meet with the pre-business adviser and discuss your interest in business school. Consider taking a course in accounting or computer science. Use the holiday season as a time to talk to recent college grads who are now in business school.

January–February

Stop by and chat with a few of the administrators. You may want to visit the alumni office and get addresses of practicing M.B.A. graduates who are in finance, marketing, and so on. Maybe your enthusiasm will convince them to meet with you and share their experiences.

March–April

Start looking for a challenging summer job. Perhaps working in an advertising firm or a brokerage house will be good experience. Work hard in your activities so that you can fill a leadership position by next year. If your school has a pre-business society, take advantage of its activities.

May–June

Try to do well on your finals and get letters of recommendation from teachers who gave you the highest grades. Talk to some seniors who have been accepted by business schools and find out what the application process was like for them.

July–August
Buy a GMAT review book and spend a few hours reviewing a sample test. If you're working in a company, try to meet some of the managers who have M.B.A. degrees. Maybe they can give you advice or later write a recommendation.

Junior Year

September
Send away to three or four business schools for catalogs and applications. Even though these are not the applications that you'll use, they're good to look over. Find out if by next year you'll have enough information to answer the questions. Ask the pre-business adviser about scholarships and loans for business schools.

October
Try to gain leadership positions in your activities. Work hard in your courses. Your junior-year grades are probably the final ones on the transcript that will be sent to the business schools.

November
Consider attending one of the M.B.A. Forums sponsored by the Graduate Management Admission Council. Review some exams in your GMAT study book. Ask the pre-business adviser for one or two past exams. Many colleges keep them on file in the career placement office.

December
Look into GMAT review courses. If you're taking the test in the spring, you may want to register for the review course now or during the next few weeks. Read through as many business-school catalogs as possible and consider the schools' size, distance, cost, level of competition, and so on.

January
Meet with your pre-business adviser and discuss the possibili-

ties of working before attending school. Also have him suggest some business schools, based on your grades.

February
Continue to study for the spring GMAT. If your college invites business-school admissions officers to campus for informational meetings, attend them and ask questions.

March
If you want to take the late spring GMAT, it is almost time to register for it. Think about next year's courses and try to select ones that will solidify the college curriculum you submit to the admissions people. Also make sure you've fulfilled your own college's course requirements.

April
Try to get as terrific and challenging a summer job as possible. It should be related to business in some way.

May
Do the best you can on final exams. Visit this semester's professors and any deans you know, and ask them for letters of recommendation. Since most students will wait until September to do this, they'll have time to write yours now. Meet with the pre-business adviser and discuss your favorite business schools. Have the adviser look at the records of students who got into those schools in the past.

June
Even if you don't know the exact business schools to which you'll be applying, send away for the new applications. They're all free, so get as many as you can.

July
If you have any free time this summer, you may want to visit a few of the business schools that interest you. Call in advance and arrange to take a tour of the campus. Try to sit in on some of the first-year classes.

August

Those of you who didn't take the late spring GMAT should register for the one given during the fall. You may want to take a GMAT review course.

Senior Year

September

Organize your applications, catalogs, and financial aid forms in a neat file and begin working on the ones that are due earliest. Make sure that you have a good selection of recommendation letters. Be certain that you understand how the system works for sending letters to schools. Some of them want *you* to send the letters while other schools want the professors to send them.

October

Meet with your pre-business adviser and narrow down your list of schools. Continue to research scholarships and other financial aid resources if you need them. When the business-school admissions people visit your campus, go to the sessions and meet them. Make an impression—sometimes they'll remember you.

November

If you took the fall GMAT, you should have your scores by the end of this month. Make a realistic judgment of your chances for admission to the schools you like. Complete all of the forms that ensure that your college transcript and GMAT scores are sent to the right schools.

December

This month is probably the last time that you can take the GMAT if you want to attend business school next year, so register as soon as possible. Try to complete all of your applications by the middle of December. The flood of applications comes in during the holidays, so try to get yours in first.

January
If you know any business-school alumni or have high-powered
contacts, ask them to help you. Since it's now or never, being
overly shy will get you nowhere. Now that your applications are
all in, you may want to contact each school and politely ask if
your file is missing anything (letters of recommendation,
transcript, GMAT scores, and so on).

February–March
Continue to look for scholarships and other sources of financial
aid. Send business schools supplementary material on any new
awards, or anything else that may help your candidacy. Keep
your grades up just in case business schools make a spot check.

April
You will probably hear sometime near the beginning of this
month. Once you've gotten in, look at the schools' placement
records. You can find them in the career services office when
you make that final visit to the business school.

Appendix

Business Schools Listed by the Graduate Management Admission Council

The following is a list of the business schools that are recognized by the Graduate Management Admission Council. In addition to giving addresses where you can write for more information, the list will tell you whether the institution is private or public. Some of the schools are independent programs that are not affiliated with larger universities.

Alabama

Alabama Agricultural and Mechanical
  University
School of Business
Normal 35762
(public)

Auburn University
School of Business
Auburn 36830
(public)

Auburn University
School of Business
Montgomery 36117
(public)

Jacksonville State University
College of Commerce and Business
  Administration
Graduate Studies
Jacksonville 36265
(public)

Samford University
School of Business
800 Lakeshore Drive
Birmingham 35209
(private)

Troy State University
School of Business and Commerce
Troy 36081
(public)

University of Alabama
School of Business
Graduate School
1016 South 15th Street
Birmingham 35294
(public)

University of Alabama
School of Graduate Studies
P.O. Box 1247
Huntsville 35807
(public)

University of Alabama
Graduate School of Business
University 35486
(public)

University of North Alabama
School of Business
Florence 35630
(public)

University of South Alabama
Graduate School
College of Business and Management
    Studies
University Boulevard
Mobile 36688
(public)

Alaska

University of Alaska
School of Business and Public Admin-
    istration
Anchorage 99504
(public)

University of Alaska
School of Management
Fairbanks 99701
(public)

Arizona

American Graduate School of Inter-
    national Management
Glendale 85306
(private)

Arizona State University
College of Business Administration
Tempe 85287
(public)

Northern Arizona University
MBA Program—College of Business
    Administration
Flagstaff 86011
(public)

University of Arizona
College of Business and Public Ad-
    ministration
Tucson 85721
(public)

Arkansas

Arkansas State University
College of Business
State University 72467
(public)

University of Arkansas
College of Business Administration
Fayetteville 72701
(public)

California

Azusa Pacific College
Division of Business Administration
Azusa 91702
(private)

California Lutheran College
Graduate Program in Business Ad-
    ministration
Thousand Oaks 91360
(private)

California Lutheran College
Graduate Program in Business Administration
Thousand Oaks 91360
(private)

California Polytechnic State University
School of Business
San Luis Obispo 93407
(public)

California State College
School of Business and Public Administration
Bakersfield 93309
(public)

California State College
School of Administration
San Bernardino 92407
(public)

California State College
School of Business Administration
Turlock 95380
(public)

California State Polytechnic University
School of Business Administration
Pomona 91768
(public)

California State University
School of Business
Chico 95929
(public)

California State University
Domingues Hills
School of Management
Carson 90747
(public)

California State University
School of Business and Administrative Sciences
Fresno 93740
(public)

California State University
School of Business Administration and Economics
Fullerton 92634
(public)

California State University
School of Business and Economics
Hayward 94542
(public)

California State University
School of Business Administration
Long Beach 90840
(public)

California State University
School of Business and Economics
Los Angeles 90032
(public)

California State University
School of Business Administration and Economics
Northridge 91330
(public)

California State University
School of Business and Public Administration
6000 J Street
Sacramento 95819
(public)

Chapman College
School of Business and Management
Orange 92666
(private)

Claremont Graduate School
Dept. of Business Administration
Claremont 91711
(private)

Golden Gate University
Graduate Programs
536 Mission Street
San Francisco 94105
(private)

Humboldt State University
School of Business and Economics
Arcata 95521
(public)

Loyola Marymount University
College of Business Administration
Los Angeles 90045
(private)

Monterey Institute of International
  Studies
425 Van Buren Street
International Management Division
Monterey 93940
(private)

Pacific State University
College of Business Administration
Los Angeles 90006
(private)

San Diego State University
College of Business Administration
San Diego 92182
(public)

San Francisco State University
School of Business
San Francisco 94132
(public)

San Jose State University
School of Business
San Jose 95192
(public)

Sonoma State University
Department of Management Studies
Rohnert Park 94928
(private)

Stanford University
Graduate School of Business
Stanford 94305
(private)

University of California
Graduate School of Business Administration
Berkeley 94720
(public)

University of California
Graduate School of Administration
Davis 95616
(public)

University of California
Graduate School of Management
Irvine 92717
(public)

University of California
Graduate School of Management
405 Hilgard Avenue
Los Angeles 90024
(public)

University of San Diego
School of Business Administration
San Diego 92110
(private)

University of San Francisco
McLaren College of Business
San Francisco 94117
(private)

University of Santa Clara
Graduate School of Business and
  Administration
Santa Clara 95053
(private)

University of Southern California
Graduate School of Business Administration
Los Angeles 90007
(private)

Whittier College
M.B.A. Program
Whittier 90608
(private)

Colorado

Colorado State University
College of Business
Fort Collins 80521
(public)

Regis College
M.B.A. Program
Denver 80221
(private)

University of Denver
Graduate School of Business and Public Management
Denver 80208
(private)

Connecticut

Fairfield University
School of Business
Fairfield 06430
(private)

Hartford Graduate Center
(affiliated with Bensselaer Polytechnic Institute)
275 Windsor Street
Hartford 06120
(private)

Quinnipiac College
School of Business
Hamden 06518
(private)

Sacred Heart University
M.B.A. Program
Bridgeport 06606
(private)

University of Bridgeport
Graduate School of Business Administration
Bridgeport 06602
(private)

University of Connecticut
School of Business Administration
Storrs 06268
(public)

University of Hartford
Barney School of Business and Public Administration
West Hartford 06117
(private)

Western Connecticut State College
Ancell School of Business
Danbury 06810
(public)

Yale University
School of Organization and Management
Box 1-A
New Haven 06520
(private)

Delaware

University of Delaware
Department of Business Administration
Newark 19711
(public)

Wilmington College
M.B.A. Program
New Castle 19720
(private)

District of Columbia

American University
Kogod College of Business Administration
Washington 20016
(private)

George Washington University
School of Government and Business Administration
Washington 20052
(private)

Georgetown University
School of Business Administration
Washington 20057
(private)

Howard University
School of Business and Public Administration
1003 K Street N.W.
Washington 20001
(private)

University of the District
of Columbia
College of Business and Public
Management
929 E Street N.W.
Washington 20004
(public)

Florida

Barry University
M.B.A. Program
Miami 33161
(private)

Florida Atlantic University
College of Business and Public
Administration
Boca Raton 33431
(public)

Florida International University
School of Business and Organizational
Sciences
Miami 33199
(public)

Florida State University
College of Business
Tallahassee 32306
(public)

Nova University
Graduate Management Programs
Fort Lauderdale 33314
(private)

Rollins College
Roy E. Crummer Graduate School of
Business
Winter Park 32789
(private)

Stetson University
School of Business Administration
DeLand 32720
(private)

University of Central Florida
College of Business Administration
Orlando 32816
(public)

University of Florida
College of Business Administration
Gainesville 32611
(public)

University of Miami
School of Business Administration
Coral Gables 33124
(private)

University of South Florida
College of Business Administration
Tampa 33620
(public)

Webber College
Graduate Studies
Babson Park 33827
(private)

Georgia

Atlanta University
Graduate School of Business Administration
Atlanta 30314
(private)

Augusta College
School of Business Administration
2500 Walton Way
Augusta 30910
(public)

Berry College
Graduate Studies in Business
Mount Berry 30149
(private)

Columbus College
University System of Georgia
School of Business
Columbus 31993
(public)

Emory University
Graduate School of Business Admin-
    istration
Atlanta 30322
(private)

Georgia College
School of Business
Milledgeville 31601
(public)

Georgia Institute of Technology
College of Management
Atlanta 30332
(public)

Georgia Southern College
School of Business
Statesboro 30460
(public)

Georgia State University
College of Business Administration
Atlanta 30303
(public)

Mercer University
Division of Business and Economics
Atlanta 30341
(private)

Savannah State College
M.B.A. Program
Savannah 31404
(public)

University of Georgia
Graduate School of Business Admin-
    istration
Athens 30602
(public)

Valdosta State College
School of Business Administration
Valdosta 31698
(public)

West Georgia College
School of Business
Carrollton 30118
(public)

Hawaii

Chaminade University of Honolulu
Master of Business Administration
3140 Waialae Avenue
Honolulu 96816
(private)

University of Hawaii at Manoa
College of Business Administration
Honolulu 96822
(public)

Idaho

Boise State University
School of Business
Boise 83725
(public)

Idaho State University
College of Business
Pocatello 83209
(public)

University of Idaho
College of Business and Economics
Moscow 83843
(public)

Illinois

Bradley University
College of Business Administration
Peoria 61625
(private)

DePaul University
Graduate School of Business
25 East Jackson Blvd.
Chicago 60604
(private)

Eastern Illinois University
School of Business
Charleston 61920
(public)

George Williams College
Dept. of Administration and Organizational Behavior
Downers Grove 60515
(private)

Governors State University
College of Business and Public Administration
Park Forest South 60466
(public)

Illinois Benedictine College
M.B.A. Program
Lisle 60532
(private)

Illinois Institute of Technology
Stuart School of Business Administration
Chicago 60616
(private)

Illinois State University
College of Business
Normal 61761
(public)

Keller Graduate School of Management
10 South Riverside Plaza
Chicago 60606
(private)

Lake Forest School of Management
Graduate School of Management
Lake Forest 60045
(private)

Lewis University
College of Business
Romeoville 60441
(private)

Loyola University
Graduate School of Business
Chicago 60611
(private)

Northern Illinois University
College of Business
DeKalb 60115
(public)

Northwestern University
J.L. Kellogg Graduate School of Management
Evanston 60201
(private)

Roosevelt University
College of Business Administration
Chicago 60605
(private)

Rosary College
Graduate School of Business
River Forest 60305
(private)

Southern Illinois University
College of Business and Administration
Carbondale 62901
(public)

Southern Illinois University
School of Business
Edwardsville 62026
(public)

University of Chicago
Graduate School of Business
Chicago 60637
(private)

University of Illinois at Chicago
College of Business Administration
Chicago 60680
(public)

University of Illinois at Urbana-Champaign
Dept. of Business Administration
Champaign 61820
(public)

Western Illinois University
College of Business
Macomb 61455
(public)

Indiana

Ball State University
College of Business
Muncie 47306
(private)

Butler University
College of Business Administration
Indianapolis 46208
(public)

Indiana Central University
Graduate Division
Indianapolis 46227
(private)

Indiana State University
School of Business
Terre Haute 47809
(public)

Indiana University
Graduate School of Business
Bloomington 47405
(public)

Indiana University at South Bend
Master of Science in Business Administration
South Bend 46634
(public)

Indiana University Northwest
Master of Science in Business Administration
Gary 46408
(public)

Indiana University—Purdue University
at Fort Wayne
Graduate Studies in Business
Fort Wayne 46805
(public)

Purdue University
Krannert Graduate School of Management
West Lafayette 47907
(public)

University of Evansville
School of Business Administration
Evansville 47702
(private)

University of Notre Dame
College of Business Administration
Notre Dame 46556
(private)

Iowa

Drake University
College of Business Administration
Des Moines 50311
(private)

St. Ambrose College
Graduate Programs in Business Administration
Davenport 52803
(private)

University of Iowa
College of Business Administration
Iowa City 52242
(public)

University of Northern Iowa
School of Business
Cedar Falls 50614
(public)

Kansas

Emporia State University
Master of Business Administration
    Program
Emporia 66801
(public)

Kansas State University
College of Business Administration
Manhattan 99506
(public)

Pittsburg State University
School of Business
Pittsburg 66762
(public)

University of Kansas
School of Business
Lawrence 66045
(public)

Wichita State University
College of Business Administration
Wichita 67208
(public)

Kentucky

Bellarmine College
M.B.A. Program
Louisville 40205
(private)

Eastern Kentucky University
College of Business
Richmond 40475
(public)

Morehead State University
School of Business and Economics
Morehead 40351
(public)

Murray State University
College of Business and Public Affairs
Murray 42071
(public)

Northern Kentucky University
M.B.A. Program
Highland Heights 41076
(public)

University of Kentucky
College of Business and Economics
Lexington 40506
(public)

University of Louisville
School of Business
Louisville 40292
(public)

Western Kentucky University
College of Business Administration
Bowling Green 42101
(public)

Louisiana

Louisiana State University in Baton
    Rouge
College of Business Administration
Baton Rouge 70803
(public)

Louisiana State University in Shreve-
    port
College of Business Administration
Shreveport 71115
(public)

Louisiana Tech University
College of Administration and Business
Ruston 71272
(public)

Loyola University of the South
College of Business Administration
New Orleans 70118
(private)

Nicholls State University
Graduate School of Business Administration
Thibodaux 70310
(public)

Northeast Louisiana University
College of Business Administration
Monroe 71209
(public)

Northwestern State University of
Louisiana
College of Business
Natchitoches 71457
(public)

Southeastern Louisiana University
M.B.A. Program
Hammond 70404
(private)

Tulane University
School of Business
New Orleans 70118
(private)

University of New Orleans
College of Business Administration
New Orleans 70148
(public)

Maine

Husson College
Graduate Studies Division
Bangor 04401
(private)

Thomas College
Graduate School of Management
Waterville 04901
(private)

University of Maine
College of Business Administration
Orono 04469
(public)

Maryland

Loyola College
School of Business and Management
Baltimore 21210
(private)

Mount Saint Mary's College
Graduate Program of Business
Emmitsburg 21727
(private)

University of Baltimore
School of Business
Baltimore 21201
(public)

University of Maryland
College of Business and Management
College Park 20742
(public)

Massachusetts

American International College
School of Business Administration
Springfield 01109
(private)

Babson College
M.B.A. Program
Wellesley 02157
(private)

Bentley College
Graduate School
Waltham 02254
(private)

Boston College
Graduate School of Management
Chestnut Hill 02167
(private)

Boston University
School of Management
Boston 02215
(private)

Clark University
Graduate School of Management
Worcester 01610
(private)

Harvard University
Graduate School of Business Administration
Boston 02163
(private)

Massachusetts Institute of Technology
Sloan School of Management
Cambridge 02139
(private)

Nichols College
Graduate School of Business Administration
Dudley 01570
(private)

Northeastern University
Graduate School of Business Administration
Boston 02115
(private)

Simmons College
Graduate School of Management
Boston 02215
(private)

Southeastern Massachusetts University
M.B.A. Program
North Dartmouth 02747
(public)

Suffolk University
School of Management
Boston 02108
(private)

University of Lowell
College of Management Science
Lowell 01854
(public)

University of Massachusetts
School of Business Administration
Amherst 01003
(public)

Western New England College
Office of Graduate Studies
Springfield 01119
(private)

Worcester Polytechnic Institute
Management Department
Worcester 01601
(private)

Michigan

Central Michigan University
School of Business Administration
Mt. Pleasant 48859
(public)

Eastern Michigan University
Graduate Business Programs
Ypsilanti 48197
(public)

Grand Valley State Colleges
F.E. Seidman College of Business and Administration
Allendale 49401
(public)

Michigan State University
Graduate School of Business Administration
East Lansing 48824
(public)

Michigan Technological University
School of Business and Engineering
  Administration
Houghton 49931
(public)

Northern Michigan University
School of Business and Management
Marquette 49855
(public)

Oakland University
School of Economics and Management
Rochester 48063
(private)

Saginaw Valley State College
School of Business and Management
University Center 48710
(public)

University of Detroit
College of Business and Administration
Detroit 48221
(private)

University of Michigan
Graduate School of Business Administration
Ann Arbor 48109
(public)

University of Michigan—Dearborn
Graduate School of Management
Dearborn 48128
(public)

University of Michigan-Flint
School of Management
Flint 48503
(public)

Wayne State University
School of Business Administration
Detroit 48202
(public)

Western Michigan University
College of Business
Kalamazoo 49008
(public)

Minnesota

College of St. Thomas
Graduate Programs in Management
St. Paul 55105
(private)

Mankato State University
College of Business
Mankato 56001
(public)

Moorhead State University
M.B.A. Program
Moorhead 56560
(public)

St. Cloud State University
College of Business
St. Cloud 56301
(public)

University of Minnesota
Graduate School of Management
Minneapolis 55455
(public)

University of Minnesota-Duluth
School of Business and Economics
Duluth 55812
(public)

Mississippi

Delta State University
School of Business Administration
Cleveland 38733
(public)

Jackson State University
Graduate School
Jackson 39217
(public)

Millsaps College
School of Management
Jackson 39210
(private)

Mississippi College
School of Business Administration
Clinton 39058
(private)

Mississippi State University
College of Business and Industry
Mississippi State 39762
(public)

University of Mississippi
School of Business Administration
University 38677
(public)

University of Southern Mississippi
College of Business Administration
Hattiesburg 39401
(public)

University of Southern Mississippi—
Gulf Coast
Graduate Business Studies
Long Beach 39560
(public)

Missouri

Avila College
Department of Business and Economics
Kansas City 64145
(private)

Central Missouri State University
College of Business and Economics
Warrensburg 64093
(public)

Drury College
Breech School of Business Administration and Economics
Springfield 65802
(private)

Lincoln University
Graduate Studies
Jefferson City 65101
(public)

Northeast Missouri State University
Division of Business
Kirksville 63501
(public)

Northwest Missouri State University
School of Business Administration
Maryville 64468
(public)

Rockhurst College
Graduate Business Division
Kansas City 64110
(private)

Saint Louis University
School of Business and Administration
St. Louis 63108
(private)

Southeast Missouri State University
College of Business
Cape Girardeau 63701
(public)

Southwest Missouri State University
School of Business
Springfield 65802
(public)

University of Missouri—Columbia
College of Business and Public Administration
Columbia 65211
(public)

University of Missouri—Kansas City
School of Administration
Kansas City 64110
(public)

University of Missouri—St. Louis
School of Business Administration
St. Louis 63121
(public)

Washington University
Graduate School of Business Administration
St. Louis 63130
(private)

Montana

University of Montana
School of Business Administration
Missoula 59812
(public)

Nebraska

Creighton University
College of Business Administration
Omaha 68178
(private)

University of Nebraska at Omaha
College of Business Administration
Omaha 68182
(public)

University of Nebraska—Lincoln
College of Business Administration
Lincoln 68588
(public)

Nevada

University of Nevada, Las Vegas
College of Business and Economics
Las Vegas 89154
(public)

University of Nevada, Reno
College of Business Administration
Reno 89557
(public)

New Hampshire

Dartmouth College
Amos Tuck School of Business Administration
Hanover 03755
(private)

New Hampshire College
Graduate School of Business
Manchester 03104
(public)

Plymouth State College
Graduate Studies
Plymouth 03264
(public)

Rivier College
Graduate Program in Business Administration
Nashua 03060
(private)

University of New Hampshire
Whittemore School of Business and Economics
Durham 03824
(public)

New Jersey

Fairleigh Dickinson University
College of Business Administration
Madison 07940
(private)

Monmouth College
School of Business Administration
West Long Branch 07764
(private)

Montclair State College
School of Business Administration
Upper Montclair 07043
(public)

Rider College
School of Business Administration
Lawrenceville 08648
(private)

Rutgers University
Graduate School of Management
Newark 07102
(public)

Rutgers University—Camden
Faculty of Business Studies
Camden 08102
(public)

Seton Hall University
Stillman School of Business
South Orange 07079
(private)

Stevens Institute of Technology
Management Science Department
Hoboken 07030
(private)

Trenton State College
School of Business
Trenton 08625
(public)

William Paterson College of New
  Jersey
School of Management
Wayne 07470
(public)

New Mexico

New Mexico Highlands University
Department of Business and Economics
Las Vegas 87701
(public)

New Mexico State University
College of Business Administration and
  Economics
Las Cruces 88003
(public)

University of New Mexico
Graduate School of Management
Albuquerque 87131
(public)

Western New Mexico University
Department of Business and Public
  Administration
Silver City 88061
(public)

New York

Adelphi University
School of Business
Garden City 11530
(private)

Bernard M. Baruch College
Graduate Studies
17 Lexington Avenue
New York 10010
(public)

Canisius College
School of Business Administration
Buffalo 14208
(private)

Clarkson College
School of Management
Potsdam 13676
(private)

College of Insurance
Business Administration Division
New York 10038
(private)

College of Saint Rose
Program in Management
Albany 12203
(private)

Columbia University
Graduate School of Business
New York 10027
(private)

Cornell University
Graduate School of Business and Public Administration
Ithaca 14853
(private)

Dowling College
M.B.A. Program
Oakdale 11769
(private)

Fordham University at Lincoln Center
Graduate School of Business Administration
New York 10023
(private)

Hofstra University
Graduate School of Business
Hempstead 11550
(private)

Long Island University
School of Business and Public Administration
Brooklyn 11201
(private)

Long Island University
C.W. Post Center
Greenvale 11548
(private)

Manhattan College
School of Business
Riverdale 10471
(private)

Marist College
Graduate Division of Management
Studies
Poughkeepsie 12601
(private)

New York Institute of Technology
Division of Business and Economics
1855 Broadway
New York 10023
(private)

New York University
Graduate School of Business Administration
New York 10006
(private)

Niagara University
College of Business Administration
Niagara University 14109
(private)

Pace University
Lubin Graduate School of Business
New York 10038
(private)

Polytechnic Institute of New York
Division of Management
Brooklyn 11201
(private)

Rensselaer Polytechnic Institute
School of Management
Troy 12181
(private)

Rochester Institute of Technology
Graduate Management Programs
Rochester 14623
(private)

St. Bonaventure University
School of Business Administration
St. Bonaventure 14778
(private)

St. John's University
College of Business Administration
Jamaica 11439
(private)

State University of New York at
Albany
School of Business
Albany 12222
(public)

State University of New York at Binghamton
School of Management
Binghamton 13901
(public)

State University of New York at Buffalo
School of Management
Buffalo 14214
(public)

State University of New York Maritime College
Dept. of Marine Transportation
Fort Schuyler
Bronx 10465
(public)

Syracuse University
School of Management
Syracuse 13210
(private)

Union College
Institute of Administration and Management
Schenectady 12308
(private)

University of Rochester
Graduate School of Management
Rochester 14627
(private)

North Carolina

Appalachian State University
College of Business
Boone 28608
(public)

Campbell University
Division of Business
Buies Creek 27506
(private)

Duke University
Fuqua School of Business
Durham 27706
(private)

East Carolina University
School of Business
Greenville 27834
(public)

Queens College
Graduate School
Charlotte 28274
(private)

University of North Carolina at Chapel Hill
Graduate School of Business Administration
Chapel Hill 27514
(public)

University of North Carolina at Charlotte
College of Business Administration
Charlotte 28223
(public)

University of North Carolina at Greensboro
School of Business and Economics
Greensboro 27412
(public)

University of North Carolina at Wilmington
School of Business Administration
Wilmington 28406
(public)

Wake Forest University
Babcock Graduate School of Management
Winston-Salem 27109
(private)

Western Carolina University
School of Business
Cullowhee 28723
(public)

North Dakota

University of North Dakota
College of Business and Public Administration
Grand Forks 58202
(public)

Ohio

Ashland College
M.B.A. Program
Ashland 44805
(private)

Bowling Green State University
College of Business Administration
Bowling Green 43403
(public)

Capital University
Graduate School of Administration
Columbus 43209
(private)

Case Western Reserve University
School of Management
Cleveland 44106
(private)

Cleveland State University
College of Business Administration
Cleveland 44115
(public)

John Carroll University
Graduate School
University Heights 44118
(private)

Kent State University
Graduate School of Management
Kent 44242
(public)

Miami University
School of Business Administration
Oxford 45056
(public)

Ohio State University
College of Administrative Science
Columbus 43210
(public)

Ohio University
College of Business Administration
Athens 45701
(public)

University of Akron
College of Business Administration
Akron 44325
(public)

University of Cincinnati
College of Business Administration
Cincinnati 45221
(public)

University of Dayton
School of Business Administration
Dayton 45469
(private)

University of Steubenville
M.B.A. Program
Steubenville 43952
(private)

University of Toledo
College of Business Administration
Toledo 43606
(public)

Wright State University
College of Business and Administration
Dayton 45435
(public)

Xavier University
Graduate School of Business
Cincinnati 45207
(private)

Youngstown State University
M.B.A. Graduate Program
Youngstown 44555
(public)

Oklahoma

Bethany Nazarene College
Division of Business
Bethany 73008
(private)

Oklahoma City University
School of Management and Business
  Sciences
Oklahoma City 73106
(public)

Oklahoma State University
College of Business Administration
Stillwater 74074
(public)

Oral Roberts University
School of Business
Tulsa 74171
(private)

University of Oklahoma
College of Business Administration
Norman 73019
(public)

University of Tulsa
College of Business Administration
Tulsa 74104
(private)

Oregon

Oregon State University
School of Business
Corvallis 97331
(public)

Portland State University
School of Business Administration
Portland 97207
(public)

Southern Oregon State College
School of Business
Ashland 97520
(public)

University of Oregon
Graduate School of Management
Eugene 97403
(public)

University of Portland
School of Business Administration
Portland 97203
(private)

Willamette University
Graduate School of Management
Salem 97301
(private)

Pennsylvania

Bloomsburg State College
School of Graduate Studies
Bloomsburg 17815
(public)

California State College
Graduate School of Business Management
California 15419
(private)

Carnegie-Mellon University
Graduate School of Industrial Administration
Pittsburgh 15213
(private)

Clarion State College
School of Business Administration
Clarion 16214
(public)

Drexel University
College of Business and Administration
Philadelphia 19104
(private)

Duquesne University
Graduate School of Business and Administration
Pittsburgh 15282
(private)

Gannon University
Graduate Program in Business Administration
Erie 16541
(private)

Indiana University of Pennsylvania
School of Business
Indiana 15705
(public)

La Roche College
Human Resources Management Program
Pittsburgh 15237
(private)

La Salle College
School of Business Administration
Philadelphia 19141
(private)

Lehigh University
College of Business and Economics
Bethlehem 18015
(private)

Marywood College
Business and Managerial Science Programs
Scranton 18509
(private)

Pennsylvania State University
Capitol Campus
Master of Administration Program
Middletown 17057
(public)

Pennsylvania State University
Graduate Programs in Business Administration
University Park 16802
(public)

Philadelphia College of Textiles and Science
M.B.A. Program
Philadelphia 19144
(private)

Robert Morris College
Graduate School
Coraopolis 15108
(private)

Saint Joseph's University
M.B.A. Program
Philadelphia 19131
(private)

Shippensburg State College
Graduate School of Business
Shippensburg 17257
(public)

Temple University
School of Business Administration
Philadelphia 19122
(public)

University of Pittsburgh
Graduate School of Business
Pittsburgh 15260
(public)

University of Scranton
School of Management
Scranton 18510
(private)

Villanova University
College of Commerce and Finance
Villanova 19085
(private)

University of Pennsylvania
Wharton School—Graduate Division
Philadelphia 19104
(private)

Widener University
Graduate Programs in Business
Chester 19013
(private)

York College of Pennsylvania
Master of Business Administration
York 17405
(private)

Puerto Rico

University of Puerto Rico
Graduate School of Business Administration
Rio Piedras 00931
(public)

Rhode Island

Bryant College
Graduate School
Smithfield 02917
(private)

Providence College
M.B.A. Program
Providence 02918
(private)

University of Rhode Island
College of Business Administration
Kingston 02881
(public)

South Carolina

The Citadel
Master of Business Administration
Charleston 29409
(private)

Clemson University
Master of Business Administration
    Program
Greenville 29613
(private)

University of South Carolina
College of Business Administration
Columbia 29208
(public)

Winthrop College
School of Business Administration
Rock Hill 29733
(private)

South Dakota

University of South Dakota
School of Business
Vermillion 57069
(public)

Tennessee

Austin Peay State University
College of Business
Clarksville 37040
(public)

East Tennessee State University
College of Business
Johnson City 37614
(public)

Memphis State University
College of Business Administration
Memphis 38152
(public)

Middle Tennessee State University
School of Business
Murfreesboro 37132
(public)

Tennessee State University
School of Business
Nashville 37203
(public)

Tennessee Technological University
Division of M.B.A. Studies
Cookeville 38501
(public)

University of Tennessee at Chattanooga
School of Business Administration
Chattanooga 37402
(public)

University of Tennessee at Martin
School of Business Administration
Martin 38238
(public)

University of Tennessee, Knoxville
College of Business Administration
Knoxville 37996
(public)

Vanderbilt University
Graduate School of Management
Nashville 37203
(private)

Texas

East Texas State University
College of Business Administration
Commerce 75428
(public)

East Texas State University at Texarkana
Department of Administrative Disciplines
Texarkana 75501
(public)

Pan American University
School of Business Administration
Edinburg 78539
(public)

Prairie View A&M University
College of Business
Prairie View 77445
(public)

Rice University
Graduate School of Administration
Houston 77251
(private)

St. Mary's University
School of Business and Administration
San Antonio 78284
(private)

Southern Methodist University
School of Business
Dallas 75275
(private)

Stephen F. Austin State University
The Graduate School
Nacogdoches 75962
(public)

Sul Ross State University
Master of Business Administration
Program
Alpine 79830
(public)

Texas A&M University
College of Business Administration
College Station 77843
(public)

Texas Christian University
M.J. Neeley School of Business
Fort Worth 76129
(private)

Texas Tech University
College of Business Administration
Lubbock 79409
(public)

Texas Woman's University
Health Care Administration Program
Dallas 75235
(public)

Trinity University—San Antonio
Master of Business Administration
San Antonio 78284
(private)

University of Dallas
Graduate School of Management
Irving 75061
(private)

University of Houston
College of Business Administration
Houston 77004
(public)

University of Houston at Clear Lake
City
School of Business and Public Administration
Houston 77058
(public)

University of St. Thomas
Cameron School of Business
Houston 77006
(private)

University of Texas at Arlington
College of Business Administration
Arlington 76019
(public)

University of Texas at Dallas
School of Management and Administrative Sciences
Dallas 75080
(public)

University of Texas at San Antonio
College of Business
San Antonio 78285
(public)

University of Texas at Tyler
School of Business Administration
Tyler 75701
(public)

West Texas State University
School of Business
Canyon 79016
(public)

Utah

Brigham Young University
Graduate School of Management
Provo 84602
(private)

University of Utah
Graduate School of Business
Salt Lake City 84112
(public)

Utah State University
College of Business
Logan 84322
(public)

Vermont

University of Vermont
School of Business Administration
Burlington 05405
(public)

Virginia

College of William and Mary
School of Business Administration
Williamsburg 23185
(private)

George Mason University
School of Business Administration
Fairfax 22030
(private)

James Madison University
School of Business
Harrisonburg 22807
(private)

Marymount College of Virginia
Graduate School of Business
Arlington 22207
(private)

Norfolk State University
Schools of Business
Norfolk 23504
(public)

Old Dominion University
School of Business Administration
Norfolk 23508
(private)

University of Richmond
School of Business
Richmond 23173
(private)

University of Virginia
Colgate Darden School of Business
    Administration
Charlottesville 22906
(public)

Virginia Commonwealth University
School of Business
Richmond 23284
(public)

Virginia Polytechnic Institute and State
    University
College of Business
Blacksburg 24061
(public)

Washington

Eastern Washington University
School of Business
Cheney 99004
(public)

Gonzaga University
School of Business Administration
Spokane 99258
(private)

Pacific Lutheran University
School of Business Administration
Tacoma 98447
(private)

Seattle University
Albers School of Business
Seattle 98122
(private)

University of Puget Sound
School of Business and Public Admin-
    istration
Tacoma 98416
(private)

University of Washington
Graduate School of Business Admin-
    istration
Seattle 98195
(public)

Washington State University
College of Business and Economics
Pullman 99164
(public)

Western Washington University
College of Business and Economics
Bellingham 98225
(public)

West Virginia

Marshall University
College of Business
Huntington 25701
(private)

West Virginia University
College of Business and Economics
Morgantown 26506
(public)

Wheeling College
M.B.A. Program
Wheeling 26003
(private)

Wisconsin

Marquette University
M.B.A. Program
Milwaukee 53233
(private)

University of Wisconsin—Eau Claire
School of Business
Eau Claire 54701
(public)

University of Wisconsin—La Crosse
College of Business Administration
La Crosse 54601
(public)

University of Wisconsin—Madison
Graduate School of Business
Madison 53706
(public)

University of Wisconsin—Milwaukee
School of Business Administration
Milwaukee 53201
(public)

University of Wisconsin—Oshkosh
College of Business Administration
Oshkosh 54901
(public)

University of Wisconsin—Whitewater
College of Business and Economics
Whitewater 53190
(public)

Wyoming

University of Wyoming
College of Commerce and Industry
Laramie 82071
(public)

Selected Bibliography

Blotnick, Srully. *The Corporate Steeplechase*. New York: Facts on File, 1984.

Fischgrund, Tom, ed. *The Insider's Guide to the Top Ten Business Schools*. Boston: Little-Brown, 1983.

Heller, Robert. *The Supermanagers*. New York: Dutton, 1984.

Henry, Fran. *Toughing It Out: A Woman MBA at Harvard*. New York: Putnam, 1983.

McCormack, Mark. *What They Don't Teach You at Harvard Business School*. New York: Bantam Books, 1984.

O'Toole, Patricia. *Corporate Messiahs*. New York: Morrow, 1984.

Peters, Thomas J., and Robert H. Waterman, Jr. *In Search of Excellence: Lessons From America's Best-Run Companies*. New York: Warner, 1983.

GMAT Review Books

Barron's How to Prepare for the Graduate Management Admission Test, 4th edition.

GMAT Preparation Guide, Cliffs.

The Graduate Management Admission Test, Monarch.

How to Prepare for the GMAT, McGraw-Hill.

About the Author

LAWRENCE GRAHAM is currently a student at Harvard Law School and the author of several books including *Conquering College Life* and *Ten Point Plan for College Acceptance*. A 1983 graduate of Princeton University, Graham has worked as student producer with NBC Studios, job and career counselor at Princeton Career Services, research assistant at the Ford Foundation, and aide for the Assistant to the President at the White House. His first books brought him nationwide recognition in *The New York Times*, *People Magazine*, *Good Housekeeping*, on the *Phil Donahue Show* and *Today Show*, and in other forms of national media. He has counseled and lectured to groups in schools, libraries and community centers around the country on college- and job-related matters.